The *Calm*
before the *Storm*

The *Calm* before the *Storm*

A STROKE SURVIVOR'S STORY

Delanie Stephenson

Edited by Erin Broughton, Brenda Lee,
Kenny Rowlette, and Dr. Alicia Zukas

iUniverse, Inc.
Bloomington

THE CALM BEFORE THE STORM
A STROKE SURVIVOR'S STORY

iUniverse books may be ordered through booksellers or by contacting:

iUniverse
1663 Liberty Drive
Bloomington, IN 47403
www.iuniverse.com
1-800-Authors (1-800-288-4677)

ISBN: 978-1-4759-9230-4 (sc)
ISBN: 978-1-4759-9232-8 (hc)
ISBN: 978-1-4759-9231-1 (e)

Library of Congress Control Number: 2013909450

Printed in the United States of America.

iUniverse rev. date: 6/25/2013

"After the storm comes a calm."
Matthew Henry

To Mommy, my mom and my best friend,
who stayed by my side; and Babe, the love
of my life, who never gave up on me

CONTENTS

ACKNOWLEDGMENTS

I would like to take this section of the book to thank the many people who helped me through this harrowing ordeal. The backing of family and friends made a huge difference in my healing process.

First of all, I would like to thank my mom, who practically moved in with me in all the different hospitals that I stayed at during the summer of 2012. She became my nurse, physical therapist, occupational therapist, speech therapist, mental therapist, confidante, and best friend. I will always treasure the talks we had during that summer. I hate that it had to happen that way, but the stroke drew us closer, and I was thankful. She was truly the lady I aspired to be. She was exactly what I needed.

I would also like to thank Curtis, my husband. Not many marriages were put to the test like ours. For better or for worse ... Curtis definitely stuck through the worst part. He stayed by my side and showed me what love really is. I was thankful for him taking care of our babies, Katie and Alex. He proved himself not only as a husband but as a dad as well.

I am also grateful to Daddy. He gave up his wife the summer of 2012 for me. He logged several hours on 460, going back and forth from home to the hospitals. He was there, holding my hand, exercising my fingers, and giving me the confidence that everything would be okay, even though I cried every time he left to go home. He always came with his shillelagh (big walking stick), on which he would get compliments, with his hip hurting, but he would never complain. He can let go of his dime now.

Susie, my mother-in-law, went way beyond the role of a mother-in-law. On Sunday afternoons, she was there working on her Sudoku book while I napped, offering her quiet encouragement. I owe her a big thank-you for opening up her home to me and my family when I first came home. I will forever be grateful. (Also, I should say thank you for the taxicab service she gave me afterward to doctors' appointments, therapy, meetings at the school for the kids, to Walmart ... the list goes on and on.)

Teresa, my sister-in-law—words couldn't describe what I need to thank her for. She helped me keep my sanity in the hospital. From telling me about her crazy family life to introducing me to *Fifty Shades of Grey* (and being my sidekick while I got my tattoo), she was always entertaining me. I never had a dull moment when she was there. I could always count on her for a good laugh. Thank you for not only being my sister-in-law but for being my friend.

To Karen, my stroke-survivor sister—I hate that I had to learn through her experience, but she was the only person I know who understood what I was going through. I always wanted to be more like her, but this was taking it to the extreme! Thank you for your words of wisdom and advice while I was going through this journey.

I would like to thank two outstanding doctors, Dr. Bekenstein and Dr. Zukas. I credit them with saving my life. They were both there from the scary start. Thank you for showing me that not only do doctors need to know their stuff, they need to care. They truly understood good bedside manner. Dr. Zukas is truly a great doctor and was, to me, a special friend. And I'm still Baptist, by the way.

The members of the Retreat staff gave me such support. I really credit them with giving me both the physical and emotional support to recover. Thank you to Mary, the awesome physical therapist whom I credited with my walking. I'm glad I could help in making your dad proud. Thank you to Linda, the occupational therapist whom I could always count on for a good laugh, and to Elizabeth, the speech therapist. Back off already! Kim and Little Kim, two of the physical therapy staff, were always making me smile. Kim, I miss your celebratory dances. Thank you also to all the nurses who took care of me in more ways than they'll ever know: Heidi, Carolyn, Rachel "The Best Nurse Ever," Natasha, Dennesha, Demetria, Matthew, Sharon, Whitney "Nurses Rock," Kristen, and many more (I couldn't remember them all); to Greg, the director of the Complex Care Unit, who believed in me and made sure I had the best care possible (and for awarding me a gold medal); and to Dr. Kuntz for watching over me at Retreat and VCU.

At VCU rehabilitation, thank you to Tracey, who was my Jillian Michaels of physical therapy; Kim, for tying me to the chair and telling me to get dressed (which I did); and Ashley, the occupational therapist intern who was constantly apologizing with me (I'm sorry, by the way).

I would also like to thank some people from Sheltering Arms: Linda, for pushing me and making me believe in myself; Gabby and Ashley, for being fun to work with and making therapy entertaining instead of a chore; Robin, for whose care and gentle touch I will always be thankful—she was so good at what she did—and Jessica, for babysitting me during the month I was there.

At HealthSouth, thank you to Allyson, for giving me the confidence to speak without being self-conscious. She made me feel like I was talking like a normal person. Thank you to Josh, for giving me the tenacity to let go of my cane and walk forward with no regrets.

I would also like to thank Stephanie, my best friend. She was the true definition of what a best friend should be. I am grateful for all of her visits, the clothes, and the talks, but mostly for her love.

To Katie and Alex, my beautiful babies, thank you for treating me like Mommy and not a stranger when I was in the hospital. All the times they climbed into bed with me, hugged me, and told me they loved me were priceless. They are my reason for living.

Thank you to everyone else I didn't mention—for all the visits, cards, balloons, and flowers. It was all appreciated. Without everyone's prayers and words of encouragement, I never would have made it through.

The Lord had a reason for this to happen to me, and if I inspire one person through this story to live life to its fullest, it will all have been totally worth it. In a weird way, I'm glad I had my stroke.

PROLOGUE

FROM A YOUNG AGE, MY parents taught me to work hard and never give up, to never settle for second best. I remember my dad having me rewrite a report I was doing in fourth grade on Martha Washington. Most parents don't expect much out of an elementary school report, but my dad, being an English professor, expected the best. One Saturday afternoon, while most kids were outside playing, he made me rewrite the paper until it was perfect. I had to write it over and over again. And this was before the days of everyone having access to computers. I was doing it all by hand. I was only in fourth grade. I got so mad at him. But it did teach me to always see things through and never settle for less than my best.

I grew up in a Christian elementary school, high school, and college. Whether I would be going to college was never a question for me. It was always just a question of where. I believed in God, got saved at the age of five, and was in church every Sunday. But somewhere along the way, I lost sight of who He was. I felt like I was being choked with all this God information. It was as if I were being told what to believe and not allowed to think for myself. I got so caught up in my day-to-day life that God was kind of placed on the back burner. I was a straight-A student (I studied as soon as I got home; I didn't talk on the phone or watch TV like a normal teenager). I was your definition of a bookworm. I didn't go to parties or have much of a social life, except for a few friends. All the hard work paid off, as I became co-valedictorian of my senior class (with a childhood friend, Christy Campbell). I walked a straight line and didn't even think of deviating from it.

While I was in high school and college, my dad and I became obsessed with Civil War reenacting. I loved history and seeing it come to life on the battlefield. While other teenage girls were going out on dates on the weekend, I would go to reenactments with my dad. He would go fight the "damn Yankees," and I would be the daughter on the side of the field, waiting to see if my dad would make it home. My dad always thought it was my love of history and the time we got to spend together that would drive me to these events, but it didn't hurt that guys were at the dances. I did have a couple of years of rebellion and dating guys that my dad didn't want me to, but in the end, I wanted to please my parents and was always seeking their approval.

My love of history followed me into college. I decided it was going to be my major. I was already involved in Civil War reenacting and was also volunteering at a local historic site, Thomas Jefferson's Poplar Forest. I was involved in the local United Daughters of the Confederacy and the Lynchburg Civil War Round Table. I even had an article published in a reenactor's magazine, *The Citizen's Companion*. It was about Robert E. Lee and his youngest child, Mildred Chile Lee. This article turned into me traveling around Virginia, doing a first-person interpretation of Mildred Lee. I had a full plate. Plus, I was working as a student worker in the history department and tried my hand at fast food, working at Dairy Queen and Chick-Fil-A. Looking back on it, I don't know how I graduated. How did I manage time to study? I was always busy, and whenever

I was at home, my nose was in a book. Again, I was walking the straight and narrow. But still, even though I went to a Christian college, God wasn't a priority.

By my junior year in college, my parents were asking me about what I was going to do for the rest of my life. They knew I loved history, but they wanted to know how I was going to make money at it. Graduate school was an option, and I dreamed of working with the Civil War Center at Virginia Tech, alongside Bud Robertson. That was my ultimate goal. They also said there was always the option of being a teacher. No way. Both my parents were teachers, and I would not follow in their footsteps. Being a researcher or working at a museum sounded nice, but there wasn't much money involved. They still wanted me to go to graduate school, get my master's in history, and see what doors opened. It was like my life was all planned out for me.

For my birthday in March 2000, my dad got us tickets to go to the Virginia Tech Civil War Institute annual Civil War Seminar. I was so excited. Here I was among history professionals. Who knew whom I would meet and what opportunities would be available? During one of the talks, I got a microphone and, in front of several hundred people, asked a panel of historians why females were not as prominent in the historical field as men. I caught the attention of the head of Pamplin Historical Park, Will Greene, from Petersburg, Virginia. I think he was impressed that a young girl, college age, would have such an interest in history. He offered me a job right on the spot. So where was I working the summer of 2000? Pamplin Park. I felt like I had made it in life. For once, I had gotten something on my own—not based on where I went to school or who my parents were. I had gotten to this station in my life by myself. Things were working out the way I wanted it for once.

I would meet my future husband that summer at Pamplin Park, but I certainly wasn't looking for anyone romantically. That summer was my first away from home, and I wanted to present myself as a professional. Love was the last thing on my mind. I didn't know what contacts I would make while I was at the park, and I was focused on my future. Besides, I already had a boyfriend at the time. That was where my attention was focused until I met long-haired, sexy-legged Curtis Stephenson. I saw him the first week and about died; I thought he was so good-looking. We were both in relationships at the time, so it was impossible for us to hang out. We found out, years later, that I was drawn to his cute legs and he was impressed at how much information I seemed to possess. Every time he saw me, my nose was in a book. My job was costumed interpretation, which consisted of getting dressed up in Civil War–era clothing and greeting visitors at an old plantation home. Every day, he would come and pretend to check on the garden that was on the grounds where I worked. He would pretend to pick onions, sit on a bench, and complain about his girlfriend. This was a good sign, I thought. He asked me to go fishing on several occasions, but I kept saying no. Finally, he broke up with his girlfriend. Things weren't working out with my current boyfriend, so I said, "Sure, I'd love to go fishing with you."

It was hard for me to concentrate my senior year in college. I wanted to focus only on Curtis. A year and a half later after we started dating, with a little bit of prodding by me, we were married. It was a small ceremony with only family. We went to Virginia Beach for one evening for our honeymoon. He had to be at work the next day, and he spent much of his time fishing while we were there. (That is another story for another book; I'm still waiting on a real honeymoon.) We lived with his mom for about three months, which was frustrating at times. They say there can't be two women in the kitchen at the same time, and that was very true. After about three months, I told Curtis, "We have to have a place of our own." His mom agreed. She was gladly giving us a gentle push out the door. We found an apartment just a few minutes from his work and settled there for a year and a half. Freedom. I was very content being on my own; Curtis hated to be cooped up. We decided to rent a trailer in Disputanta, Virginia. It was small, but it was out in the country.

Curtis could build a fire, mow grass, and hunt behind the house. He could escape. He loved it. But we were renting, and I felt that we needed a place that was ours since we were throwing our money away. Through much pushing (Curtis takes things very slowly), we found eighteen acres in Wilsons, Virginia. This was the place that we would call home. I became a history teacher at Hopewell High School (I never should have said I would never be a teacher) and spent eleven wonderful years there. There were some frustrations and many principals, some better than others, but I loved the students and the people I worked with. My husband gave me a daughter, Katie Elizabeth, on November 22, 2005. Curtis Stephenson Jr. (Alex) came August 9, 2007. As a family, we had our ups and our downs, but all in all, I'd say we lived a pretty good life. Besides, nothing could go wrong. We were living the American dream, and what could mess that up?

At the high school, my goal was to bring history alive for young people. They had to take history and pass a Standard of Learning test in order to graduate, so they didn't have a choice in taking the class. I remembered how boring some of my high school and college professors were, and I wanted to be different for the students I taught. I won't say that I was an expert my first year (ask some of my former students … I wasn't), but like everything else, things got better with time. I learned to communicate to the students to where learning was fun. I worked in what I would call an underprivileged school (most kids were on free/reduced lunch, where they paid little for it or got it for free), many of their parents were into drugs, and it was not uncommon for some of my freshman girls to either be pregnant or already be moms. Many of these kids were dealing with a lot outside of school. The last thing on their minds was world history. I soon found out that if I could relate the history to them in a way that they could understand it in twenty-first-century lingo, they would get it. I made them work hard. I had many children who would come back to me a year or two after having them and tell me they wished I would move up a grade or two so I could teach them again. History might not have been their favorite subject, but at least I was able to make it tolerable.

I had my family life and work life under control. God and church were still important to me, but I didn't go as much as was expected of me. It was just too hard to get up early on Sunday mornings. I would get up and exercise at 4:30 a.m. all week long. We would make an occasional appearance on Easter or Christmas, but we weren't "spiritual" by any means. I would pray when something big was going on in my life that I needed help with, but not on a daily basis. I kept my relationship with God very much to myself and was not very vocal. I knew the importance of raising my kids in a church family, and maybe it was the rebel in me to not go. My parents had been on me for years to go to church, but I saw it more as nagging than anything else. God, like so many other things in life, had been crammed down to the bottom of the pile of important things to do.

All throughout my life, I've been a people pleaser and a *big* worrier (to the point of being annoying). I worked hard at my marriage, at being a mom, at work, and in life in general. I would always try to give my friends a call so I wouldn't lose touch with them, give Curtis intimate texts at lunch to keep it interesting, make sure my kids were involved in activities, and try to be home for every holiday or birthday. Sometimes, when I was trying to make everyone else happy, I forgot about myself. My life was very stressful. Whose isn't? Go here; go there; pay bills on time … Again, God would make an appearance when I needed Him. I thought I could do everything on my own. I would get mad at my kids and my husband over the stupidest stuff. I thought I had my priorities straight, but I didn't. Something would happen to put all these things into perspective.

LIFE BEFORE

IT WAS THE WEEKEND BEFORE Alex's fourth birthday, and we decided to have his party in the local bowling alley. Most of the people there were family. Kids had fun "trying" to bowl and playing video games. My mom and dad, my sister Karen, and her two boys were in attendance along with several aunts, uncles, and cousins. The birthday cake was good, the fellowship even better. My sister and I were looking really good. We had both recently lost weight and had a golden hue from the summer on our skin. We took pictures, and everyone had a good time. That was on Saturday, August, 6, 2011. On Monday, August 8, Karen was to have a scheduled procedure at the hospital to have a benign mass on her neck removed. I honestly forgot about it that Monday until my mom called later that day. I always wish I had called my sister that Monday morning to hear the old Karen one more time.

As of August 10, 2011, my life would never be the same. As I said, my sister had gone into the hospital for routine surgery to have a mass removed from her neck, and they accidentally snipped the carotid artery on the right-hand side. It turned out that the mass was congenital, meaning it had been there since birth, and the carotid artery was wrapped all around it. They had to tie the artery off. She would have only one working carotid artery (she was supposed to have two: one on each side of her neck). There was some serious bleeding because of this, and she almost bled to death. I knew she was going to be in the hospital longer than expected. My mom told me that the doctors almost lost her on the operating table. When she was in the recovery room, she was all by herself; her husband wasn't even by her side. The nurses told her how close to death she had come. She cried, overtaken with emotions, and she had no one to share them with. Her husband finally made it to her side when she was more stable. He was able to share in her feelings of anxiousness.

Karen's neck was swollen from the procedure. She was having trouble swallowing, and they didn't want to let her out of the hospital until she was eating well. We figured it was due to the swelling after the surgery. She couldn't swallow anything properly, and the nurses were afraid she would aspirate if the food or drink went down the wrong way. My mom told me this, and I was baffled. I didn't know there was a correct way to swallow; I just did it. She ate some applesauce, and they thought it was good-enough proof that she could go. Here she was, near death, could barely get any food down, and the hospital released her as if nothing was wrong. When she got home, she sat in her recliner. She got out her laptop and logged into Facebook. Karen typed, "Home☺," on her status. Her husband went upstairs to take a shower. Then it happened. Thankfully, my mom was there; she saw Karen slump over. Karen was feeling some numbness and tingling, and they almost had to drag her back to the hospital. She didn't want to go back, but they didn't give her a choice.

I had just put the kids in bed and put on my nightgown when my dad called around 8:30 p.m. and said, "Delanie, Karen had a stroke. We are in the emergency room at Lynchburg General. No need to come down. Just pray." I dropped the phone in disbelief. Strokes were something that happened to the elderly, not twenty-nine-year-olds who were in great shape. Karen had been married to Ben for seven years, had two young kids, ages four and two at the time, was a great English teacher, had recently lost a significant amount of weight, and had the rest of her life ahead of her. Stroke? No, someone must have it wrong.

Since my dad told me not to come back to Lynchburg, I headed back to Lynchburg. I lived about two hours away; it was about nine o'clock at night. My husband, Curtis, told me not to worry about the kids and just go. I didn't even think. I put some clothes on—I didn't pack anything, not even a toothbrush—and hopped in the van. I thought for sure that Karen would be fine, and I would head back to my own home later that night.

As I was going down 460 West, everything was a blur. I felt like I was living a nightmare. I called my mom to tell her I was coming and to be on the lookout for me. She tried to settle me down and told me Karen was comfortably waiting on a bed in the ER. I didn't calm down. I was scared. I called my best friend, Stephanie. I knew it was too late to call, but I did anyway. She told me she would pray and for me to let her know what was going on. I don't really remember the two-hour drive home. My mind was just racing. When had I last told my sister I loved her? What about her kids? I imagined Karen in a wheelchair for the rest of her life, not being able to walk. Was she going to have to depend on her husband for everything? How was she going to cope? Driving down a lonely road for two hours gave me too much time to think. For a worrier, this was not a good thing.

I finally pulled up in the parking lot of the hospital ER—I don't even know how I got there—and was running my way inside. When I saw my dad outside the ER doors waiting for me, I burst into tears. "Why?" I asked. "Why did this have to happen to Karen?" He assured me that Karen was okay and then walked me inside. When I saw my mom in the waiting room, I started crying again. She told me Karen was okay and they were just waiting to run some tests and admit her to a room. I wanted to go see her, but my mom said I needed to calm down first. I had to be strong for Karen. The last thing she needed to see was a splotchy-faced, blubbering idiot standing by her bed. I finally got it together and promised myself that I wouldn't cry in front of her. My mom walked me back to where she was. She was sitting up in bed, with her husband and father-in-law laughing at her side. She had her right leg propped up, and she gave me a wave. I could see her neck was swollen from where they had done the surgery, but for the most part, she looked like plain old Karen. Her voice was a little hoarse, but she seemed okay. *Stroke,* I thought, *they must have it wrong.* I was actually a little relieved.

I had seen Karen in the hospital a few times before. I saw her in the hospital when I was about ten and she was seven. They put her in the hospital because she was dehydrated. When I saw her with an IV in her at such a young age, I thought it was the worst thing ever and actually started crying it bothered me so much. Karen had said, "What is she crying about?" She never let on that she was scared. She gave birth to two boys, Ty and Jack, so I had seen her when she was in the hospital with both of them. It made sense then; she had a purpose for being in the hospital. Karen had always been able to put a strong face on. I was the weaker sibling. And that was what she was doing now, putting on a brave face for all of us so we would be able to smile back at her like everything was okay. But on the inside, Karen was scared to death. The word *stroke* is something a person doesn't take lightly. No one in our immediate family had experienced one, except for my paternal great-grandfather and he died from his. With that thought in her head, she didn't want to admit it, but death was staring her in the face.

They wound up keeping Karen in the ICU overnight. My mom, dad, and I stayed in the waiting room while her husband went home and took care of a few things. I fell asleep on one of the couches, and Daddy did also, reading a magazine. Mommy did her usual thing when she was nervous; her leg was shaking at warp speed until Ben got back. Ben stayed the night with Karen, and the rest of us took the quiet trip back to my parents' house. It was after midnight, and my mom didn't want me to drive back to my house alone. We were all trying to soak up the day. We were living a nightmare. I climbed into bed in my old bedroom. I don't think any of us did much sleeping that night. I thought about happier times with Karen. At that point in time, no one mentioned the word *stroke* again.

The next morning, my mom decided to go back to the hospital while my dad and I stayed at the house. Karen's sister-in-law was going to drop Karen's boys off at my parents'. My mom said she would call from the hospital if anything happened. The day went by pretty uneventfully. Ty and Jack played, Ty with his beloved trains, and Jack stood too close to the TV (he would later need glasses). My dad and I tried to take a nap that afternoon, and my godparents dropped off soup for me to fix for supper. Stephanie dropped by too, offering her support, and I tried to feed and take care of the kids the best I could. I kept bugging my husband, calling him and asking how my kids, Katie and Alex, five and four at the time, were doing. My dad and I ate, joking about old times and wondering when my mom would be home. She hated cold food. My dad was getting a little annoyed that she wasn't home yet, so he decided to give her a call. I checked on the boys to make sure they were okay, and my dad looked at me after he got off the phone, his face as white as a sheet. "They think Karen's blood clot is spreading and getting more massive in her brain. I have to get to the hospital fast," he said.

I looked at him in disbelief. This was something you watched in a Lifetime movie, not real life. I stayed at my parents' house to watch the boys. Jack went to bed easily, and Ty was amused with train shows, which he watched over and over again. I kept waiting to hear something from my parents, but no news came. I kept thinking, *No news is good news, right?* Wrong. My dad called and said that the blood clot in the brain kept spreading. I didn't know what to do, but I felt like I needed to do something. So I turned my mom's laptop on and signed into Facebook. I updated my status with everything that was happening. Every time my mom or dad would call with an update, I would post it on Facebook for the world to see. People I hadn't heard from in years came to light, wishing Karen the best and offering up their prayers. I kept one ear out for my cell phone and my face glued to the computer screen as my sister's Facebook wall blew up in front of me. My mom, who was against Facebook before this, was grateful for the website because it let us get the word out about Karen so much faster.

Ty was oblivious to what was going on, and he finally went to sleep. I kept pacing the floor, waiting for the next phone call with an update. My dad prepared me for the worst, saying the next twenty-four hours were critical. There was nothing left to be done. The prayer chain was started, and all we could do was wait. My parents made it home around midnight. I left the computer on, and my mom saw Karen's face on the screen. It was a picture of Karen literally taken a few days before at my son's fourth birthday party. Karen looked so happy. My mom saw what I was doing and what nice things people were writing, and she broke down in my arms. I don't think I'd ever seen her cry like that before. It was like I was the parent and she was the child.

We all went to bed, pretending like we were going to get some sleep. I tossed and turned all night. My mind would not rest. I kept thinking about these two young boys—Who was going to take care of them if something happened to Karen? Finally, the darkness turned into the predawn hours. It was decided my mom would go back to the hospital for the morning while my dad and I waited for Karen's sisters-in-law to pick up the boys again. It seemed like the morning dragged on for forever. Finally, around noon, the girls came for the boys, and my dad and I headed to the hospital, not knowing what waited for us there.

We met my mom in the waiting room. She was pacing back and forth, which was not a good sign, and one by one, we were allowed to see Karen. I was shocked by what I saw. There were so many tubes and IVs in her arms. She was doped up with so much medication. I tried to hold it together. I couldn't lose it in front of her. She could barely lift her hand to acknowledge I was there. She was totally paralyzed on the left side, we were told. This once boisterous young lady had shriveled up into almost a vegetable overnight. I didn't know what to say or what to do while I was in her ICU room. I sat down in a chair beside her. The TV was turned to HSN, and I teased her that she was trying to buy stuff while she was in the hospital. She didn't laugh, which was so not like Karen. I stayed for a few minutes and then left so she could rest. After a while, another person would go in and spend a little bit of time with her. It was like that all afternoon. Many well-wishers came by—Karen's friends and people from church. I felt numb; Karen did literally.

I was going home that afternoon since my son had an important battery of tests for the seizure issues he'd been having for a few years. I was going to come back the following week to spend some time with Karen and, I hoped, see some progress. As I walked into the little ICU room to say good-bye, I really had to try hard to hold back the tears. I wondered whether or not I would see Karen again. I told her I loved her and would be back soon, but I don't think she heard me. She just closed her eyes and went back to her drug-induced state. My parents walked me out into the parking as I was getting ready to leave, and tears streamed down my face once more. I said my good-byes and headed home with promises of returning soon.

The ride back home was even shorter than the drive down. I called everyone imaginable to let them know what was going on if they hadn't already heard via Facebook. I honestly don't remember the two-hour drive home. Before I knew it, I was pulling into my gravel driveway. I went inside, saw my husband and two kids, and lost it again. I had a lot to be thankful for.

The next morning, I woke up and called my parents to check up on Karen. It was more of the same with no improvements. I had been exercising to Jillian Michaels since my birthday earlier that year. Karen actually gave me the DVD for my birthday. I had two choices, get on the Ben and Jerry's diet downfall, or continue with my exercise regimen. I had a moment of WWKD (What would Karen do?) and went forward with the workout. As I started exercising, I was crying—not in pain, but in the realization that Karen might never get to exercise again. Karen might not be there tomorrow. As my husband entered the room, he looked at me like I was crazy. "Crying while you are working out?" he said.

"I'm working out in honor of Karen," I shot back. As cheesy as it sounded, I was doing just that.

I felt so helpless at home. I felt like I should be doing something. My husband and I brainstormed, and then a friend from school gave me a great idea to set up a Caring Bridge web page in Karen's honor. It sounded great. Caring Bridge was a free website set up for people to keep informed on how a loved one or friend is doing during a serious health condition. I could put pictures on there and update how Karen was doing, and there was even a guestbook where people could encourage Karen. All afternoon, my heart and soul was in that website. I posted pictures of Karen, Ben, and the boys and told her story and background. By the end of the day, the website had over four hundred hits. I could tell Karen was loved.

The next week flew by, kind of in a haze. My days consisted of calling my parents, finding out Karen's status, and then posting the update onto the website I had set up for her. Hundreds of friends were sending their well wishes on the guestbook and on Facebook. I slept with the cell phone by my bed in case my mom called in the middle of the night. People from all over the world were commenting. They were all saying the same thing: they were dumbfounded that something like this could happen to someone so young. It made no sense.

Later that week, Karen was moved from the ICU into a regular hospital room. I visited again, not knowing what to expect. Many of Ben's family members were already present in the room, and what I heard and saw was awesome. She was talking, smiling, and laughing, kind of like the old Karen. Her speech wasn't the same; it was low and raspy, and her smile was a little different, but she was there. I saw flickers of my baby sister. Somehow, she was going to make it through this thing.

The fall of 2011, Karen worked the hardest she ever had in her life in rehab. She lost a lot of weight because she couldn't eat regular food. She couldn't swallow her food or drink properly, so she had a PEG (feeding) tube inserted in her stomach. My mom became her caregiver, coming by every day after work and spending time with her. Her husband, Ben, would sleep in a cot by her bed; she hated to be alone at night. Many events took place in that rehabilitation center. Karen learned to talk louder, sit again, stand again, and walk again! She worked hard on a daily basis, aching to get home to her husband and kids. She had her son Jack's second birthday in the rehab center. She couldn't eat a piece of the birthday cake. My family would come down as much as we could and visit her. I remember her sitting in a chair; she had to be strapped in because she couldn't even sit up straight. This broke my heart. Alex didn't mind visiting Karen; he saw it as another place to play. Katie was a bit taken aback by everything. She didn't like seeing her aunt Karen in a hospital bed. This wasn't the Karen she knew.

Karen's ultimate goal was to get out by her birthday on October 15. She got out October 14, 2011. We had a small celebration at her house, with just family, for her birthday and homecoming. It was small and quiet, not like the birthday celebrations we were used to Karen having. Karen was big on celebrating any event.

Karen's work was not done. She would go to rehab, two or three days a week, my mom acting as chauffeur. My dad would often come with her just to spend time with her. When her insurance said they were not going to pay any more, donations were made and checks were written to make sure she could receive the most therapy possible.

Then came Thanksgiving and Christmas 2011. The holidays weren't bad, just different. Fall and the holidays were Karen's favorite times of the year, and she just wasn't into any of them. Without Karen's spunky personality, they weren't the same.

Winter turned into spring 2012. Everyone in our family was determined to make 2012 a better year. Karen was walking with a cane. She had not regained the use of her left arm, but she seemed happier. I could often see glimpses of the old Karen coming out, especially in her humorous personality. She was a bit timid at first of going out in public, but slowly, she made appearances. First, she slipped into church. She sat in the back. Next came girl nights with her friends, first at her house and then out in public places. She went on her first "date" with her husband, Ben. She went to Walmart with my mom (one that was thirty miles away so she wouldn't see anyone she knew). I could see the progress every time I came to visit; slowly, she was coming out of her shell. We would all now go to Walmart in town. We went to the mall and the grocery store. Yes, Karen was disabled, but she was learning to accept her new life.

One thing that was very hard for Karen was the fact that she had to give up her privilege to drive. While she was in the hospital, her license expired. Medically and legally, she couldn't get behind the wheel. This was probably one of the biggest setbacks she had to deal with. She had to go places when other people could take her. She sometimes couldn't go when and where she wanted to go. Karen was on someone else's schedule, which was extremely frustrating to her. Even though she had to get others to drive her, she was able to get out and around.

I remember the first time she came to my house in March 2012; I was so excited. It felt like it was Christmas. She hadn't been to my house since August 2011, the weekend before everything happened. I fixed one of her favorite meals, baked spaghetti, and was delighted just with the fact that she was in my home. She came to my daughter's dance recitals; one was in December 2011 and another in May 2012. She even insisted on helping out with my daughter's hair for the spring recital. We went to see a play and saw her son, Ty, graduate from preschool; things were looking up. Maybe it was going to be all right for the Rowlette/Beatty/Stephenson families in 2012.

But I missed the old Karen. She would call and talk to me on the phone every once in a while, but it wasn't the same. Karen often referred to someone having a stroke as if it were like losing a loved one. And it was true. The outer, physical shell was still Karen, but the personality wasn't. I missed the Karen who would call and talk about nothing, go shopping until she dropped, and always be on the go. Now, she spent her days in her basement, on her cell phone, kind of removed from the outside world. She would go out with her friends and went to a stroke support group every once in a while, but I didn't really understand what had happened to Karen on the inside.

It had gotten to June 2012 and Karen's oldest son, Ty, was graduating from preschool. We attended his graduation. I had had a bad headache the whole week prior. Like Karen before her stroke, I had lost seventy-five pounds over the past year and was in the best shape of my life. I exercised every day and watched what I ate. I didn't even think anything bad would happen to me. Normally, if I had a headache, I would just take two Tylenol. But the headaches kept happening for a week. They got so bad that at the end of the day, my whole neck was stiff. I would get my husband to massage my neck at night; it was unbearable. My mom told me to buy a cervical pillow. She said this because she always had neck problems and the pillow helped her.

June 4, 2012, was a proud day for my husband and me. My son, Alex, graduated preschool and was heading off to kindergarten in the fall. (He was about the same age as Ty.) We took pictures of him in his cap and gown. There was a great picture of the three of us, Curtis, Alex, and me. It was the last picture taken of me where I would consider myself "normal." We looked so happy. Curtis took Alex fishing that day as a reward. Things in my family were great at the time. Yes, life was stressful, but we were content. But that headache kept nagging me. It made an appearance the day of Alex's graduation, and I thought maybe a long nap would help. It didn't. I told Curtis that if it still hurt by Friday, I would go to the doctor. That was on Monday. Daily, the headache would get worse, and by lunchtime, I would be in tears because of the pain. I had experienced bad sinus headaches and headaches during a cold, but nothing like this. The pain was in the back of my head, at the base of the neck. I should have known something was up. By Wednesday, June 6, 2012, the headache got serious, and my life would change forever ...

Chapter 2

THE DAY MY WORLD CHANGED

JUNE 6, 2012, STARTED LIKE any other day. I got up at 4:30 a.m. and did my Jillian Michaels workout. I showered, got ready, and then got my husband and kids ready to go. We were out the door by 6:00 a.m. and off to start another day at our various locations. I had a normal day at school filled with complaints from the students about reviewing for the SOLs (Standards of Learning tests), which were the following week. They didn't want to do any of the work in general. After all, it was June and my students were done with school, at least in their minds. Throughout the day, my headache got worse, like it had been doing for the past week, and I texted my husband at lunchtime telling him that my head really hurt. It wasn't like any other headache I'd ever had. I made it through the day, and luckily my last period of teaching (we taught three eighty-minute periods and were off one) was planning, where I would plan for the next day. I could rest a little bit. I left feeling satisfied that I had gotten through another day of high school freshmen without going crazy.

That meant it was a good day. I got in my van and set off to pick up my son from day care.

When I got to day care, the director pulled me to the side and said she had some concerns about my son, Alex. She thought he was developmentally not prepared for kindergarten. She thought it might be good to hold him back for a year. This was after they had a graduation ceremony two days before. I nodded my head, pretending I was listening to her, knowing good and well my son was going to kindergarten in the fall. When I got back in the van and headed home, I called my husband and discussed what the day-care director had told me, and he agreed with me that we would go ahead and send him on to "big school," as we called it. My husband told me I was a worrywart and everything would be okay. As I've said, I always worried and stressed out about everything. As I drove down the road, all I could think about was my son. The more I thought about it, the more stressed out I got. It was a forty-five-minute drive home, and I had a lot of time to think. My headache got worse.

I got home and piddled around the house for a few minutes while my son watched some SpongeBob. I drove down the driveway to get my daughter, Katie, off the bus. I called my mom to discuss the situation with Alex and my concerns, but that was when Katie's bus pulled up. I told my mom I would call her later. Katie got in the van, and I headed back to the house. I decided to let the kids play outside while I cleaned out all the trash in my van. Two kids meant that it was always in a state of disarray. I went inside, got a garbage bag, and proceeded to start cleaning out the van. I sat in the driver's side as my kids continued to play. My husband was making a stop on the way home, so he wasn't there at the time.

All of a sudden, my body felt funny. A wave of nausea swept over me. I started sweating profusely and thought I was getting the start of a stomach bug. Then the left side of my body felt all tingly. I rested my head on the steering wheel and closed my eyes for a few minutes. I thought that if I could just rest, it would all go away. But it didn't.

I slumped over the steering wheel and listened to the kids playing in the background. After a few minutes, I knew I was not fine. Now my left side was tingling *and* numb. I thought I might be having a heart attack. Luckily, my cell phone was in the car. I picked it up and quickly dialed my husband's number. There were many occasions where my husband would not answer the phone for various reasons. I had been a victim of that on several occasions (mostly during fishing and hunting seasons) and prayed to God that he would pick up. He did. I told him to hurry home because something was wrong with me. He told me to stay put. Luckily, he was only about five minutes away. I kept him on the phone, talking to me, and he told me to calm down until he got home. The sound of his wheels on the driveway was like music to my ears.

By now, Katie had noticed something wasn't right. She kept asking, "Mommy, are you okay?" and I wouldn't answer because I honestly didn't know; I didn't want to scare her. My husband started asking me, "How do you feel? What does it feel like?" and I told him I felt sick to my stomach and could feel nothing on my left side. By then, I was literally soaked with sweat. He decided to take me to the hospital. He loaded the kids in the van and then sped down the highway toward Petersburg. Curtis just had a look of shock on his face. He was concerned, but he didn't want to let on because of the kids. The kids didn't realize the seriousness of the situation; they were chattering in the back of the van like it was a normal outing.

That thirty-minute drive to the hospital was the longest thirty minutes of my life. I could feel my body slowing down and my soul getting ready to leave it. I kept praying "God, help me please!" I wanted to be sure I was going to heaven; Curtis was going ninety miles per hour down the highway. This was one time I didn't get on him for speeding. He called his mom and told her what was going on, and she said she would meet us at the hospital. At that point in time, I didn't filter the words coming out of my mouth. I kept feeling myself slip away. My heart was beating so fast, and I yelled out, "This is it. I'm going to die." I felt as if death was something that was inevitable. Curtis told me to quiet down so I wouldn't frighten the kids, but I kept saying it over and over. My vision was getting blurry, and my body started to writhe in weird positions; my hands and legs were moving in different directions, and I couldn't control them. I would stiffen, and then my body would relax. It repeated this process over and over. I felt like I had really a bad Charlie horse. That was the scariest thing of all, not being able to control my body.

After what seemed like an eternity, we pulled up to the emergency room of Southside Regional Hospital in Petersburg. My husband ran inside to get some help, and they came out with a wheelchair. I couldn't move. I couldn't even make it out of the van. Katie was upset to see me in that state and kept yelling, "What's wrong with Mommy? Leave her alone!" The poor thing didn't know what was going on. When the ER staff realized that a wheelchair wouldn't work, they brought out the gurney. Somehow, they were able to transport me on there and strap me down. I vaguely remember seeing my mother-in-law with a kid in both hands out of the corner of my eye, and I was thinking, *Take care of my babies*, as they wheeled me away. Would I ever see them again? I hadn't told them that I loved them. I tried to yell, "I love you," but nothing would come out.

As I was taken inside the hospital, several members of the ER staff were wheeling me down a long hallway asking my husband a million questions. "When did she start feeling like this? Where is she numb? Was she saying anything on the way to the hospital?" Curtis was befuddled and nervous, I'm sure, answering the questions as well as anybody who was in that situation could. I don't remember what any of them looked like except for one. She called my name many times. She had long, curly dark hair. I have no idea what her name was. My body kept tensing up. My arms were constricting (*posturing*, I would later be told it was called), and my legs were going in all different directions. All of a sudden, it hit me what was happening to me and visions of my sister flashed in my head. I was having a stroke.

I tried to yell out, "Stroke!" but what came out of my mouth sounded more like a caveman grunting than any type of human voice. It was like a growl or a groan. This was not the way I normally sounded. This sounded inhuman, like a rabid animal. I tried yelling it again, thinking that if they knew what was happening, they would be able to fix me. But much to my dismay, it sounded all guttural and incomprehensible. All the while, the ER staff was saying, "Delanie, can you hear me? Delanie! Delanie!" I watched as the ceiling lights were flashing before my eyes, and I felt like I was on the TV show, *ER*. They finally got me into a trauma room and started cutting my clothes off of me. I thought, *Oh goodness. I hope I shaved my legs and have pretty underwear on. Strangers are going to see me naked.* Priorities, priorities.

They were putting all kinds of probes on me. They laid me on another bed. I was hoping I had shaved my armpits that day when someone mentioned that I was on my period. I had forgotten to stop by the drugstore and get my birth control prescription refilled the day before. I made a mental note to do that on the way home because I was sure I wouldn't be in the hospital long. I was still in denial that something bad was happening to me. Someone put a catheter in, which didn't hurt like I expected it to, and from what I understand, they were able to give me a shot of TPA, or the "clot buster" drug as many doctors would often refer to it. It could only be given within a few hours of a stroke, which was why it was so important Curtis gave them a time frame of when all this happened. All of a sudden, it was like I woke up from a nightmare, and I started coming to. My arms and legs were no longer moving in a crazy manner. I could talk normally. I asked to see Curtis. The clot buster had worked.

My husband and mother-in-law came into the room and seemed relieved to see me doing okay. They asked me how I felt. Of all things, I was worried about the Dooney and Burke pocketbook that Curtis had gotten me for Christmas, and I was not satisfied until I knew where it was. My mother-in-law, Susie, asked me what had happened, and I proceeded to tell her the series of events I remembered between home and the hospital.

For a good ten minutes, everything was okay. I was feeling fine. I was talking normally. I was so ready to get out of there. Then all of a sudden, my speech became a little bit slurred. I didn't feel quite right. Curtis and Susie looked at me, wondering what was going on. I started to writhe without control again. I thought, *I thought they fixed me?* I would later learn that the TPA, the life-saving drug they had given me, had caused some hemorrhaging to occur in the right side of my brain. I was posturing terribly, and the ER staff rushed into the room again. This time, I started grunting, groaning, and foaming at the mouth. It was like I had rabies. I had no control over my entire body again. It did whatever it wanted to do, and I couldn't stop it. Someone yelled, "She's throwing up!" and leaned my head to the side. They wiped off my mouth as I continued to twist and turn. I continued to throw up, and they turned my head to the side so I wouldn't aspirate. This went on for about ten minutes, and for the second time that day, I thought, *I am really going to die.* I prepared myself the best I could and then closed my eyes, deciding not to fight it anymore. At least if I died, I wouldn't have to suffer.

I'd heard of people having out-of-body experiences before. Every time I would hear about it on a talk show or news special, I would think those people were crazy. But I felt myself leave my body and hover over the room. It was like I was looking down from the ceiling, as a spirit, looking down as they worked on my earthly body. Again, I prayed to God that I hadn't gotten saved at the age of five for nothing and He would let me in to paradise. I was still making the grunting noises and foaming at the mouth, but things were slowing down. It was like I was in slow motion. I thought, maybe if I just gave in, closed my eyes, and got ready for my eternal sleep, it would be easier than dealing with the situation at hand. Then I thought of my kids, my husband, my parents, and my sister. How would they do without me there? Would Curtis be able to handle the kids and the day-to-day struggle that being a parent entailed? What would it be like for my parents to bury their oldest child? What were the odds that this would happen to Karen and me?

As all of this was going on, I kept hearing, "Delanie! Delanie!" I tried to ignore it, but the voice kept bugging me. I was trying to bat the sound away so I could just drift off. "Delanie!" Then I realized that it was two female members of the ER staff calling my name. Something told me to look at them, and I focused on their faces a little more. They were a little blurry at first, but gradually, I was able to see them fully. I realized I was not dead. I was back in my body again. I would still posture and make animal grunts every once in a while, but the sounds were not as bad as before. I was alive.

Somewhere, while all of this was happening, it was decided that I needed to be transferred to VCU Medical Center for more detailed observation and more tests. They put me in an ambulance while I continued to posture. I remember the rescue worker in the back of the ambulance. He would hold me down when I would go through one of my writhing periods, which were now happening about every five minutes. I would jerk around on the gurney. He kept telling me, "You have to stop doing that," and not in a friendly way. He would even shout out, "Oh no, here she goes again!" like I was an inconvenience to him. It would come and go. One minute I was lying still, and the next, I would have one of my episodes. Again, my body would stiffen and then relax. It was such a relief when it did. It felt like my body did the day after a good workout, and my muscles were sore and worn out.

It took forever to get to VCU. Every stoplight seemed to stay on red. I felt every bump on the road. Finally, we reached my intended destination, and I was removed from the ambulance. Again, they whisked me down another long hallway with new ER staff. I really didn't know what to expect. I do remember thinking, *More people are going to see me naked.*

Then everything went dark.

Chapter 3

THE FIRST DAY OF THE REST OF MY NEW LIFE

APPARENTLY, I HAD A VERY eventful night, but I was unaware of it. My husband had called my mom and told her what had happened earlier in the evening—just the part about me going to the hospital. She had spent the day with my sister and her kids and was trying to get them settled. When my husband called, my mom said her hands were tied up and she would call him back in a little while. This was not too long after I had called her about Alex. I had said I would call her back. She got so wrapped up in helping my sister and her boys that she forgot to call. As she headed home to her house, she got to thinking, *I'd better call Curtis.* When she called again, Curtis told her that I was in bad shape, I was being transported to a hospital in Richmond, and everyone in his immediate family was already there or on the way. She took this to mean "Get up here *now!*" But he never mentioned the word *stroke* to her.

My mom and dad hopped in their car, without packing anything, and headed to Richmond. On the ride up there, my parents were dumbfounded. Yes, something serious was going on with me. I was in the hospital, but they thought surely I would be fine. They thought surely this would be a short trip. Never in a million years did my mom and dad think that not one, but two, of their daughters, would have strokes. What were the odds?

Apparently, while I was out of it, doctors did CT scans, MRIs, and all sorts of tests to be sure that it was a stroke and determine how much damage had been done to the brain. They decided to intubate me because I wouldn't stay still. I kept writhing. I remember having a dream. I felt like I was covered in bedsheets. I felt smothered in them and couldn't get out. I kept wiggling, trying to break free. This was when all the testing was going on. After studying the tests, the neurologists came to the conclusion again that I had had a major brainstem stroke, and the shot of TPA had caused hemorrhaging (bleeding) on the right side of my brain. The brain stem controlled my breathing, blood pressure, heart rate, speaking, swallowing, and emotions—practically everything. If I was going to have a stroke, I went full out. My entire left side was paralyzed. Two new people were introduced into my family's life, Dr. Bekenstein and Dr. Zukas, whom I would not meet until later. They knew everything about my situation. To this day, I credit them with saving my life. Other doctors might have given up on me, but they didn't.

Although the doctors were taking extreme care of me, they had to be honest with my family. *If* I survived the night, my life would be totally different. I might be locked in, meaning I would only be able to move my eyes and nothing else. I wouldn't be able to talk, walk, or move anything but my eyes back and forth. I might not even be able to smile. This stunned everyone. My husband, who didn't cry much, was wiping the tears off his face. He didn't deserve this. It was not fair to him, to anyone.

I was put on the regular ICU unit because there were no beds available in the neurology ICU. I would stay there for the first night. My family was staying in the ICU waiting room. Susie and Curtis's sister Teresa stayed until about 2:00 a.m. Curtis's brother Charles and his wife were taking care of the kids. My parents stayed. Curtis wouldn't even talk about leaving. I imagine that they were scared to death with the unknown lying before them. At least I was having a good long nap.

The first thing I remember when I came to was being in a dark room with little light and my family near me. My eyes opened, and my mom, Karen, my sister-in-law Teresa, and my niece Ashley were all standing around me. They were all praying and crying. I was thinking, *What in the world is going on?* I didn't understand all the events that had taken place. They each took a turn praying, holding my hands, tears overflowing as they did. I was able to turn my head a little to my mom and give her a questioning look. I couldn't talk because I still had the breathing tube down my throat. I didn't know where I was or what was going on. The room seemed dark and menacing. My mom told me to look at her, so I did. This made them all cry even more. I was thinking, *I just moved my head. What's the big deal?* She told me to squeeze her hand, which I proceeded to do as well. Everyone was wailing by then. Why was everyone looking at me with long faces? What happened to me?

My mom was stroking my hair and finally explained to me that I had just suffered a stroke. I thought, *You've got to be kidding.* She proceeded to tell me I might not walk or talk again, which sent me into a state of shock. I started to cry. My mom used to say I was not a pretty crier. I was one of those people whose face broke out in splotches and scrunched all up—not exactly a pretty sight. But my mom later told me it was the most beautiful cry she had ever seen. The doctor said I might not even make movements again, and I had already moved my head, squeezed my mom's hand, and moved my facial muscles. Dr. Bekenstein gave my mom a thumbs-up and said, "Way to go, Dr. Mom." From that point on, I was determined to prove them wrong.

I really don't remember anything until Friday, June 8. I was focused on the fact I had only five sick days at work that I hadn't used. There would only be a few days left unpaid until the end of the school year. Who worries about that at a time like this? I later learned that someone from school left a message on my cell phone and asked me if I was going to come to work or not (this was the *day* after I had the stroke). I was extremely groggy and vaguely aware of what was going on. I remember my mom and dad in the room, along with Curtis, Susie, Teresa, and Karen. I felt everyone was staring at me. It was an odd feeling to have a million thoughts running through my mind and not be able to express any of them. I constantly scanned the room. When I would make eye contact with my sister, she would give me a look of empathy that said, "Delanie, I know how you feel." She had literally been in the situation before. She was the one person who could relate to what was going on. She knew how it felt not to be in control of her body and not to be able to do anything about it. She had already had almost a year of dealing with her stroke, and now I had to deal with my own stroke setbacks. Sometimes it was better to be the patient. No one knew what was going through my head, so as a person on the outside looking in, she was really at a loss for what to do. My brain wouldn't stop.

I was still on a ventilator, so my only option was to listen to people talk. That was probably the hardest thing out of the entire situation. My mind was totally intact. I was thinking normally and was fully aware of what was going on but was not able to communicate with anybody. Conversations were going on, and I could not join in. That drove me out of my mind. Teresa, who always brought fun to any situation, was doing her best to lighten the mood. She washed my hair, gave me facials, put lotion all over my legs and feet, put makeup on me, and painted my fingernails and toenails. It was like being at a spa. I think she felt like something needed to be done to take my mind off the situation, and she did her best to beautify me. She did all she could to make me feel comfortable.

Visitors would come and go. Some of Curtis's cousins came; his aunt and uncle came. The local pastor and his wife stopped by. Most of the people who came to visit me were members of Curtis's extended family, the Stephensons. I always knew they were nice and had enjoyed the time I had spent with them in the past, but I was kind of shocked at how concerned and loving they were to me at this time. They would hold my hand, stroke my hair, and give me a kiss on the cheek. This made me feel like they cared. I was grateful for their visits. I looked at them like I was listening as they spoke, but I was tired, so tired. It wore me out to have any visitors. I don't remember much of the visits early on. The medication I was on made me tired, and all I wanted to do was sleep, but that was hard to do with a roomful of people. I was thirsty; my mouth was dry from my breathing tube. I wanted a drink of water, but there was no way I could tell that to anybody. All I could do was stay in the hospital bed, trapped in my mind.

There were a couple of visitors who stuck out from the rest: Teresa and her cousin Janie. When those two got together, there was no telling what could happen. I had met Janie several times before. She was nice and very pretty, but I had never really been close to her. When she first came in, I was honestly surprised to see her. She gave me a hug and a kiss, and I remembered her perfume. She smelled so good. She and Teresa were always making me laugh. I can't remember what they were talking about, but I was actually able to giggle when they were around. (That was hard to do with a breathing tube in and my mouth clamped tight around it.) There was a time when I was laughing so hard, Teresa was worried my mom would get mad at her for getting me so wound up. My heart rate went up from laughing so hard, and my mom told me to settle down. But I was thankful for the silliness. Teresa and Janie would make me laugh until my sides hurt. I looked forward to the times they would come see me. They would always make me feel good about myself. Like a human being. It allowed me to forget about where I was and what had happened to me. For a little while.

On Saturday, three of my aunts on my mom's side—Trina, Judy, and Peggy—and my grandmother Edwards, my mom's mother, came by. They had traveled ten hours to see me. I still couldn't talk to them. The breathing tube was still in. That was killing me, not being able to express myself. I was a teacher and an extreme talker, so this was like torture. I remember my grandmother, her eyes full of worry, holding my hand and trying to tell me everything would be okay. My aunts and my mom were having conversations, but again, I couldn't join in. I don't remember what they were talking about. I was supposed to get a dog from Aunt Trina during the summer. I was making a trip to a family get-together in southwestern Virginia on June 25. The stroke threw a wrench in that. Trina promised me she would keep ahold of the dog until I was well enough to get it, which I honestly thought would be sooner rather than later. My aunts gave me hugs, kissed my cheek, and offered me words of encouragement. I was strong, and I could make it through this. All I could do was nod in agreement. My grandmother looked like it hurt to see her granddaughter in a situation like this. I guarantee she was thinking that she'd rather be lying in the hospital bed than have me there. I'll never forget the look in her eyes. It was a look of pity and sadness. She wanted to do something to fix the situation, but there was nothing she could do.

Sunday was a big day for me. The respiratory specialists were pleased with my breathing and oxygen levels enough to where they were talking about removing my breathing tube. I was so happy at the idea of being able to talk again. My jaw hurt from my teeth biting down on the breathing tube. I wanted it out so badly; I didn't even think about it hurting. That afternoon, a respiratory specialist came in to remove the tube. He said I would feel a gagging sensation when he pulled the tube out. I didn't know how far down the breathing tube went. He said, "One, two, three," and he pulled it out. It literally felt like my intestines were being pulled out of my mouth. It was more surprising than painful. At last, I was free. They watched me extremely closely for the rest of the day to make sure I was breathing properly. All I did was concentrate on my chest going in and out, making sure I was still breathing.

I wasn't as happy as I thought I would be. I could barely talk. It was not very loud or understandable. My teeth were still clenched as if the breathing tube were still in. Nurses said that was normal; my mouth had been in that position for four days. I told myself that in a few days' time my voice would return to normal. My throat was irritated. I thought I would be able to have something to eat that evening. But to my surprise, I wasn't swallowing properly. Wasn't swallowing properly? I was swallowing my spit. Then I noticed I was drooling more than usual. Maybe it was harder to swallow than I thought. I remembered Karen and all the therapy and swallowing tests she had to go through in order to eat normal food again. It was months before she was eating just applesauce and yogurt. This would be a longer process than I thought.

That evening, as I dozed in and out, I could see Teresa, Susie, and Curtis talking. It was hard to make out what they were saying, but I could tell they were talking about money. I surely couldn't return to work for the rest of the school year, and who knew when/ if I would be able to return to work in the future? They were talking about bank statements, short-term disability, insurance, Social Security disability, all things that I would have normally taken care of. I wanted so badly to join in, but I just didn't have the strength or voice to do so. Teresa said something about finding my checkbook in my purse and seeing how much money was in my account. That got me a little angry. I didn't like the fact that they were talking about Curtis's and my finances without me, but what could I do? I realized someone had to take care of the bills and other financial obligations. Curtis hated paperwork, so Teresa was the one who got to handle all that. It was out of my hands.

I knew I should focus on regaining my strength, but I was a person who liked control. Curtis would always get on me for being in "teacher mode" when I came home. He would often remind me that he was not one of my students. What bothered me was the lack of control. At this point, I couldn't do all the things that needed to be done. I knew I would have to give that all up for a time, and I didn't know if I could.

As Sunday night came upon us, it was decided Curtis would get a break and my mom would stay in the hospital with me. I was in for a long night. I was having a hard time getting out all the fluid that had built up in my lungs from the breathing tube. It was like having a chest cold and trying to get out all the phlegm. This was going to take more than Mucinex. I coughed like I had pneumonia. They had to keep my bed at a certain angle so I wasn't lying flat to prevent further fluid in the lungs. I had a suction tube they gave me, and that helped to get some of the mucus that was getting backed up in my mouth. I would get choked up and have to use the suction tube to help me breathe. I was struggling with this the whole night. I had a nice young nurse that evening. She was cute with blonde hair and took good care of me. She sat my bed straight up trying to help, but it didn't. She even turned the bed into a massage chair type of device. The bed would vibrate back and forth for about fifteen minutes. I thought my insides were going to be shaken out. It was like when the doctor told me to pat my babies on the back to break up a bad cough. It didn't help at all. I would nod off and then go into a coughing fit. My mom and I didn't get much sleep that night.

As Monday morning arrived, I still couldn't say much. It was still more of a grunt. I was getting frustrated. I would try to say something, and my mom would think I was saying one thing when I really meant something else. I had a ton of worries on my mind, and I couldn't talk about them with anyone. I was scared. Nobody knew because I couldn't tell them. Teresa bought me white boards with magnetic alphabet pieces little kids played with, thinking I could spell out what I was trying to say. That didn't work either because I didn't have the strength even to move the letters on the board or I couldn't lift my right hand up high enough to grip the letters and spell out any words. I was getting at my wits' end just trying to communicate with people. I started to cry. So many thoughts that I couldn't share with anybody.

Why was this happening to me? What did I do to deserve this? I had two lovely kids and a loving husband who would have major changes in their lives if I didn't get any better. I might lose them.

My children hadn't seen me in a few days and were staying with relatives. I had never been away from them for long. I was always there to tuck them in to bed and tell them good night. I was there when they woke up in the morning. If I wasn't there for a long period of time, would they forget who I was? Tears started streaming down my cheeks, and with all the power my vocal cords would allow me, I said the one place that I wanted to go, "Home!" It didn't sound like my normal voice, but at least it was a voice. It sounded clear. People could understand me. I said "Home" a few more times. I proceeded to say "Babe, Katie, and Alex," the three most important people in my life, as loudly as I could, and my mom knew what I was saying. My mom and Susie were standing by my bed, and they were crying too. They were happy because they hadn't known if I would be able to say anything understandable again. (I think I scared my mother-in-law a little. I had always been able to keep my emotions in check around her, and I really cried that day.)

My mom called Curtis and told him what I had said. He was elated. Then she called my dad and my grandmother. It was like a parent whose child had just spoken her first word. It was truly a miracle. Everyone was relieved that I was saying something. This gave all of us hope—hope that if I could make little baby steps like this, maybe after a period of time, other things would come back as well, hope that I might return to the life that I used to live, hope that one day, I would return to the place that I desperately wanted to go: home. That afternoon, I cried a lot just so I could speak. Crying seemed to give me a voice.

I was still certain that this was a short-term situation, and I would be on my feet in no time. I was in for a surprise.

Chapter 4

THE CALM BEFORE THE STORM

MY FIRST WEEK IN THE ICU was predictable. Around 7:00 a.m., doctors would make their rounds asking me what the date was, where I was, who was president, and what happened to me. I answered these questions to the best of my ability. I would get tired of these questions before I left the hospital. I had to answer them so many times. I was asked to move my eyes up and down and from side to side (which I couldn't do). My eyes didn't go all the way to the left or right. I had double vision, so it was hard to look anyone in the eye. I was told to touch my nose and then the doctor's finger with my right hand and repeat it several times. I did poorly performing these simple tests. My hand was very shaky, and I couldn't lift my arm that high. I kind of forgot the doctors' faces in all the hubbub. But there were two that stuck out to me: Dr. Bekenstein and Dr. Zukas.

Every time Dr. Bekenstein would come in, he would have a smile on his face and would hold my hand and ask me how I was doing. He never talked down to me; I comprehended everything he said. He spoke in plain English when he was describing what was going on, not "doctorese," which I couldn't understand. He did the same tests on me, moving the eyes and lifting the right arm, and every time he saw the slightest bit of improvement, he would praise me and act like I had gone miles since the last time he had seen me. I liked him. He assured me that one day, I would be back to normal. He just couldn't tell me when.

Then, a young woman with short hair and glasses came in, Dr. Zukas. She had a very calm demeanor about her and was soft-spoken as she asked me questions and told me information. I felt like I had a lot in common with this lady. She was my age and asked me questions about world history (which was what I taught). She never stayed long, but I enjoyed her company. I grew to like her and looked forward to her visits. I knew her conversations were testing my cognitive abilities, but I felt like we were just having a good conversation. She didn't feel like a doctor; she felt like an old friend.

It was finally decided that my catheter would be taken out. The same cute, blonde-haired nurse was taking care of me that particular day, and she convinced me to sit in a chair. That sounded like an easy task, but it was difficult since I couldn't walk. She went to get this contraption that looked like a genie lift (which is pretty much what it was). They were able to get a harness up under me and connect me with straps to this machine. Slowly, I went up in the air. (They compared it to a ride at an amusement park, but I didn't see it.) They wheeled me over to the chair and let me down easily. I was surprised that my head wouldn't stay put. I couldn't keep it straight, and I felt like a rag doll. It kept leaning to the right. In fact, my whole upper body was leaning to the right—another side effect of the stroke. This put a strain on the left side of my neck since my head couldn't support itself. My neck muscles really felt uncomfortable. After she positioned many pillows around me, I finally was somewhat comfortable (not really). It was the first time I had been out of the bed in five days.

While I was sitting in the chair, the nurse came by and said she was ready to pull out the catheter. I don't really remember how they put it in, but I was nervous about how they were going to take it out. Without any prior warning, she reached up my hospital gown, and pop went the tube. It didn't hurt; it was more of a relief to have it out. I couldn't believe what she had just done. After about thirty minutes in the chair, I was tired and ready to get back in bed. They got me in the same way they got me out—by hoisting me on the genie lift—and they had to support my head as it hung limp.

At this point in time, I had a million IVs in me giving me fluids. I even had one in my neck where they administered most of my medication. They wanted to make sure I didn't dehydrate since I couldn't drink anything. All of a sudden, because of all the fluids, I felt the urge to pee. Normally, this would not be an issue. I would just go to the bathroom and take care of my business. I had not had to worry about the issue when the catheter was in for several days. The catheter was out now, and if I needed to go, I needed to do it properly. But what was properly at this point? I knew there was no way I was going to make it to the toilet. I couldn't walk. What were the nurses going to do? Carry me to the toilet? I wasn't even sure if I could sit up straight without slipping off. That left only one option: the bedpan. I panicked. I had never used one before but had read about them in books. From what I knew about them, they were pretty uncomfortable. I also didn't know how I was going to get on one. I decided to hold the urge as long as possible. When I felt like I was going to burst, I got my mom's attention and said something that sounded like "pee." She didn't understand me. I pointed down there with a worried look on my face, and my mom understood. She went to get the nurse.

When the nurse and my mom came back, the nurse was holding this yellow, odd-shaped thing. *I'm supposed to go in that?* I quickly learned the bedpan roll. They had me roll to the left (I couldn't roll to the right), they stuck the bedpan underneath me, and then I rolled back onto the bedpan. Tada, the bedpan roll. (I would get really good at this before the summer was over.) Now to use the bedpan. I learned that going in front of an audience wasn't going to happen. I got stage fright. I couldn't go. Not with the nurse standing right beside me. I looked at my mom, and she picked up on it. It was taking me a long time to do my business. She asked the nurse to give me a little bit of privacy, and the nurse told me to let them know when I was done. I felt like I was in elementary school. I had to ask the teacher if I could go.

The art of using the bedpan had not been mastered yet. When I finally concentrated and relaxed enough, I decided to give it a go. Ahhhh ... what a relief. But to my surprise, nothing went in the bedpan. Instead, it went up and over it. I was going like a boy, my mom said. The nurse came back and asked, "What happened?" My mom and I just kind of looked at each other. She got me cleaned up and put new bedsheets and a new gown on me, and finally, visitors could start to come in. I hoped I wouldn't have to do that for a *long* time.

That afternoon, my first physical therapist came in. I think his name was Jim, but honestly, I don't remember. He said we were going to sit in the chair again, but without the aid of the genie lift. I thought to myself, *What? How am I going to do that?* With his help, I sat up in the bed. I hadn't sat up without back support since the prior Wednesday. A full week without sitting up and now I would have to almost unsupported. I didn't know what to expect. I soon realized that I couldn't sit up right. I would start leaning to the right and feel like I was going to fall over, and then he would easily push me back up. My back was all slouched over, and I couldn't keep it straight without his support. He stressed the need for good posture. My hair was a mess, and I was drooling. I couldn't even control my own spit. What was up with that? I imagined myself in a nursing home, with Curtis coming to visit me while I was in a catatonic state. This was a true fear of mine. I thought I might be more messed up than I had originally thought. If I couldn't even hold my head straight, this was pretty serious.

Jim said we were going to do a little dance to the chair. Sure enough, with much of his guidance, he stood me up, and I swiveled on my right foot while he hugged me and inched me over to the chair, which was about two feet away. I couldn't believe I stood. All the weight was on my right leg, but I did it. I got into the chair without the machine. I was a little dizzy and nauseous, but it was so good to get out of that bed again. Curtis had come back by this time, as well as my dad and other family members, so I enjoyed sitting and listening to them talk. I couldn't really handle any long conversations since my voice would give out quickly. But my dad supplied me with plenty of laughter. I felt like I was part of the human race again. My dad had me laughing so much that I pooped in the chair from giggling so much. He was almost as bad as Teresa. I was embarrassed that the physical therapist found out about this, but what was I going to do, sit in it all day? He got me cleaned up and acted like it was no big deal.

After about an hour, I was super tired and got back in bed. It was well into the afternoon. Naptime. People stayed until about 7:00 p.m. and then said their good-byes. It was time for the night shift to begin. Curtis was staying with me again and watched TV. I tried to watch it too, but the double vision made it hard for me to concentrate. Around 9:00 p.m., we drifted off. Around midnight, I was awakened for more medicine. *Hey, lady,* I thought, *I'm trying to sleep.* Nights in the hospital were long, and there was no place to get rest. They left the lights on and had loud voices; there was a lot of laughter as the nurses had their own conversations, and machines were beeping all the time. How was listening to the sound of my heart rate supposed to give me a good night's sleep? What if I heard it stop?

Sometime in the night, I woke up with the sudden urge to use the bathroom. Then I realized something, how could I get ahold of the nurse? I couldn't just call out loudly enough for her to hear me. Curtis had fallen asleep with the call bell on his lap, and I couldn't get his attention either. I tried throwing a stuffed panda bear that the kids had gotten me at him, but the throw was totally off course.

The panda barely made it off the bed. I started crying. I had to pee, and no one could help me. A task that had seemed so simple before had become a monumental problem. I did the only thing I could do. I wet the bed.

I hadn't done that since I was a little girl. I was embarrassed. I tried calling for the nurse. "Help! Help!" I called, but what I was saying didn't sound like "help." Finally, one of the nurses heard me and saw what I had done. She cleaned me up, saying, "That's all right; we'll get this all taken care of in no time." No time meant wiping me up, changing the sheets, and getting me a new gown. Then she left as if this were normal, while I lay there horrified. Curtis slept through it all in the recliner beside me, snoring away. I tried to go back to sleep, but when I woke up in the middle of the night in a hospital, it was like time stood still. The clock hands moved so slowly, and it seemed like forever before morning came.

Morning did come. And with it came more of the same—family visitors, conversations around me, bedpan, medication, point to my nose, and so on. I was becoming accustomed to life in a hospital. One thing I realized was that I couldn't eat. Food hadn't been my top priority for a while. Survival was. I didn't realize I hadn't eaten until someone mentioned it to me. "Have you eaten since the stroke?" and all of a sudden, I was hungry. I hadn't eaten in over a week. I still had the swallowing issue, so Chick-Fil-A, which was conveniently located downstairs in the hospital, was not even an option. I was getting bored. My mom could tell by the look on my face, and she asked me if I wanted to get in the chair again. I nodded yes. They brought the crane back in and got me ready to get in the chair. Normally, getting in the chair was fine, but when the nurses hoisted me in the air this time, something was different.

I started to feel really dizzy and nauseous, and the world around me seemed to be in a fog. My head felt heavy, and I was tingly all over. It was all I could do to make it into the chair. I thought, *Something's not right. I feel like I'm going to die again.* Everything was in a fog. I felt that if I made it to the chair and sat down and rested, I would be okay. My heart was pounding; I felt my pulse racing. They finally brought me down, and I still wasn't quite right. The nurses didn't notice a thing about me. They actually left the room. My mom looked at me and could tell by the look on my face something was wrong. She kept asking me, "Are you okay? How do you feel?" It took all the energy I had to shake my head no. Nothing came out when I tried to speak. Not even a grunt. My heart rate increased abnormally high on the monitor, and my mom ran for the nurse, the same one who had put me in the chair. The nurse complained that she wasn't going to get me in and out of the chair all day and said something had better be wrong with me. If I got back in bed, I was going to stay in bed. My mom gave her an ice-cold look. That was the one and only time during my whole hospital stay where my mom got mad at a nurse.

I finally was put back in bed, still not feeling quite right, and of all times, the speech pathologist came in. My mom tried to explain to him that something was wrong and I wouldn't be able to work with him at the moment, but he didn't seem to care. He asked me to go "Ah" and "Uh," but when I opened my mouth, nothing came out. I felt like I was in a stupor. My body felt weak, and I was still lightheaded. The speech therapist thought I was being stubborn and left. He said he couldn't work with me if I had an attitude. He didn't understand. A rehab doctor came in and started asking me some questions. At this time, my mom had gone to get help. My heart rate on the monitor skyrocketed to 130. The rehab doctor kept questioning me, and I just stared at him. I couldn't verbally answer anything he was saying. I don't think I was comprehending the conversation at this point. This was the first time since the initial stroke that I had felt funny in the hospital. My mom rushed back with a nurse, and I started posturing my arms again like I had when I had the initial stroke. I thought, *Oh no, here we go again.* My heart was racing, and everyone was looking at me with concern. Dr. Bekenstein was called at this point to check in on me. He seemed concerned as well. It had seemed like forever, but the whole situation only lasted about fifteen minutes. Finally, I started to come out of my fog. I stopped posturing, and my heart rate slowed down. I could somewhat move again and make some noises out of my mouth. Everyone seemed to calm down. I was okay. Dr. Bekenstein ordered an EEG to make sure everything was fine. He was convinced I had had a seizure and put me on seizure medication.

Later that afternoon, a woman came by to do the EEG. While she was putting gook and probes in my hair, I lay back and took a nap. I was very familiar with EEGs since my son had had to have several for his seizures. I just snored away. I know my mom was a little shaken up, as was the nurse who had complained about putting me back in bed earlier. I took it as an opportunity to get some rest.

All that afternoon, I had several visitors. My mom was still a little worried, but you couldn't tell anything was wrong with me (except for the fact that I'd had a stroke). Many of the people who came were former colleagues I had taught with. They were teasing me on how I did whatever I could to get out of school early. I had fun reminiscing about old times at work. Everything was going to be okay. I was out of the woods. Or so I thought.

Chapter 5

MOVING DAY!

IT WAS FINALLY DECIDED THAT Curtis needed to go back to work. I may have had a stroke, but life around me had moved on. That was one thing I had learned since I had my stroke. My world might slow down, but everybody else's didn't. Curtis's boss called him and told him, very nicely, that if he wanted to keep his job, he needed to come back on Friday, which was a week and a half after I had entered the hospital. That meant that on Thursday, he had to go home, get a shower, and get his thoughts in order for the day of work ahead. This was a very hard moment for us. As he came to say good-bye to me, I got scared. He had been by my side since day one, and he was my comfort zone. When he left, I wouldn't know what he was doing, where he was going, anything about him. He was my one piece of normal in this whole situation. All of a sudden, I had a big fear of him leaving me for good. I mean, who could blame him? He had a wife who might not talk or walk again and couldn't clean his house or cook his meals; I didn't know if I could even do my wifely duties anymore. I felt helpless. I actually told him that he needed to find a better woman who could fulfill his needs. He said he would have none of that. I started crying; he started crying. It was a long good-bye. As he left, he took one last look at me, with tears in his eyes.

He was gone. Would I see him again? Would I see my kids again? I relayed these fears to my mom in broken sentences, and she said not even to think about that. But they were real fears. How many times had I watched a Lifetime movie where the wife had a terminal illness and the husband found love in the arms of another woman? I watched too much TV.

The same day, my best friend from childhood, and one of the only people I'd kept up with from high school, Stephanie, and her husband, Jon, came to see me. This helped keep my mind off Curtis leaving. We met in gym class in tenth grade and wound up discussing Luke Perry from the film *8 Seconds*; we'd been friends ever since. She'd come from about two hours away to see me. It was the first time she had been away from her newborn baby. She left him, which is a scary thing to do for a first-time mother, for me. We chatted, to the best of my ability, about fashion, celebrities, gossip, and all the things girls talk about. I think Jon was bored out of his mind. I really don't think they understood half of what I said. My throat was hurting so bad from the strain I was putting on my vocal cords. When I tried to say something, they would just nod their heads and say yes or no, even if what I said didn't require a yes-or-no response. They would look at me all glass-eyed, like "I have no idea what she's saying," but they wanted me to think they did. This tended to be the practice of many visitors. Conversations included lots of nodding. It finally came time for Stephanie to leave, and she didn't have to say anything. I'd scared her. She thought she might have lost her best friend. We just held hands and cried for a few minutes, and then she got up and left. I cried some more. Everybody was leaving that day. Curtis, Stephanie ... who was next?

One evening during that week, I was able to experience a hospital specialty: the sponge bath. I had heard about them before, but like the bedpan situation, I had never experienced one. A nurse came in and said she was going to clean me up so I would feel better. That didn't sound so bad. It had been over a week since I'd had a shower, and I was feeling pretty grimy. I was okay with the situation until she started undressing me. I had learned by then there was not much privacy in a hospital setting, but I didn't know how little. She totally undressed me head to toe, and I was lying there completely naked. I had experienced a little of this fear of people seeing me naked earlier when I first entered the hospital in Petersburg and at VCU, but I had been in trauma then. Now I could really comprehend what was going on. She was very gentle and cleaned me everywhere—and I mean *everywhere*. That was kind of weird. But when she was done and dried me off, I have to admit, I felt better. Fresh sheets and a clean gown could put anyone in a better mood. This was just my first of many experiences with the sponge bath.

The rest of the week was pretty much the same. Doctors' rounds were at 7:00 a.m., nurses would usually give me a bath, and then visitors started coming around 9:00 a.m. Nurses were in and out all day administering medicine. I would usually take a nap in the afternoons and enjoy conversation until dinnertime when people would start to leave. I would go to sleep around 8:00 p.m. Like I said before, the nights seemed to drag on forever. Mr. No-Nonsense speech therapist came back a few times. We didn't get too far in our work together. Dr. Bekenstein came by almost daily to check up on me. I enjoyed seeing him. I swear he never took a day off. Another favorite as I mentioned earlier was Dr. Zukas. I took a liking to her from the start. She would ask me questions; for example, she would hold up a pen and ask, "What is this used for?" She quickly understood that everything was okay with me mentally; it was the physical part that wasn't working the way it was supposed to. She was the first doctor to seem to get me. My dad and I were talking one day, and she came in to assess me. She told me to say three words: *Episcopalian*, *Methodist*, and *Catholic*. It sounded easy, but it wasn't. I repeated and said, "Episcopalian, Methodist, Catholic," and added in "Baptist" (which was what I was). My dad and Dr. Zukas burst out laughing. This would become a running joke with us. Every time she came in the room, I would say those three words and add in there "Baptist."

Another interesting point in the week was the insertion of the feeding tube. It had been about a week since I had eaten, and the doctors didn't want to go longer without me getting nutrients in my body. I knew that getting the feeding tube inserted would be awful because I had heard about Karen's, so I prepared myself for the pain. The same nurse who had complained about me getting in and out of the chair earlier that week (and had made my mom so mad) was awarded the task of putting the feeding tube in, much to my mom's and my delight. It was not very pleasant. Why didn't they numb me for some of that? She took a long, skinny tube and stuck it up my nose until it hit the back of my throat and headed down my esophagus toward my stomach. She used a machine, similar to an ultrasound, to make sure the tube was going the right way. But the tube kept getting stuck. She tried to guide the feeding the tube over and over, but it wasn't going the way it was supposed to. For some reason, it kept getting off track; something was blocking it. This made me gag. It didn't help that she was pulling the tube in and out, trying to find the right direction. This caused an unexpected reaction. I sneezed all over her. I didn't mean to; it was just a reflex. She said people threw up while getting the procedure done, but no one had ever sneezed in her face. She decided to give up and let another nurse attempt it a couple of hours later. My nostrils needed a break. That afternoon, a new nurse put it in. No problem.

After a week in the ICU, I was told I would be moving to a step-down room. This was not considered a regular hospital room; it was a step down from the ICU. Instead of constantly watching me, the nurse would be in every couple of hours for an assessment. This was a move in the right direction. I was told I would spend a few days in this room and then go to inpatient rehabilitation to start learning to do basic human functions again (walking, talking, swallowing, et cetera). *This is doable,* I thought. *I can handle this.*

Late one Tuesday evening, I was rolled down to my new surroundings. This was a part of the hospital I had never been to before. I expected something like a hospital room I would see on TV: a nice private room with a view. It didn't even cross my mind that I might be sharing it with anyone. And I had no view. I didn't have a window to look out of. It was like a closet. We could hardly fit Curtis and me in there when we drew the curtain. Each room housed two people. Luckily, the person in my room was being discharged, so it was just me for the moment. One TV per room. How does that work with two people? Teresa, Janie, and Susie were there with me at this time. Boy, was that a situation. Teresa and Janie were there. Together. They were trying to decorate the limited space I had. They were making comments about how small the room was and how ghetto it looked and were making me laugh until my stomach hurt. They had taken the pictures Teresa had made while I was in the ICU to decorate my room, and she and Janie were trying to decide where everything needed to go.

While this was going on, there was another more personal situation that needed to be addressed, soon. I hadn't had a bowel movement for several days. I told this to the nurse, and she gave me a suppository (I wasn't scared; I'd have many before I went home). She said to hold it in as long as I could and it would work better. Ten minutes later, I had to go. I told Teresa, and she tried to find the bedpan in the hospital room. That was an adventure. She and Janie looked high and low for one. They tried the bathroom, and all they could find was something that looked like a shovel for a litter box. We finally called for the nurse, and she said that the litter box shovel was the bedpan. That didn't look like it would hold anything. Teresa said they needed to reinvent the bedpan. Couldn't it at least be pink in color instead of the seventies yellow? I said, "Get out. I gotta go."

I tried to go but had no success. I was feeling terribly constipated. Everybody left around 5:00 p.m. I looked at Curtis, and he looked at me; I thought, *This has got to be a joke, right?* I was constipated in a bed that was too small for me. It was hot, and I couldn't get comfortable. I was completely miserable. I couldn't just get up and walk out of there. I was in some extreme pain (I thought it was gas). I thought if I sat on the toilet, it would be easier to go. Gravity could do its job. I said, "Toilet," to Curtis. He didn't get it. "Toilet," I said again. He still didn't understand. I pointed toward the bathroom. Finally, he got it, and he looked at me like I was crazy. He wasn't going to take me to the toilet in the condition I was in. He wasn't going to be the one responsible for me falling flat on my face. I kept saying, "Toilet," and crying out. My stomach hurt. Tears were coming down my cheeks, but Curtis was going to stand his ground. No toilet for me. My mom and dad came by at this time, and I tried to get my dad to take me to the bathroom. I was a daddy's girl, and he usually gave in. Surely, he would do something as simple as taking me to the bathroom. Nope. Even he wouldn't take me.

My parents left, and I finally calmed down enough to doze off for a little while. Around 10:00 p.m. (hospitals have weird hours), I was told I was going to be transferred to a private room. Hallelujah. We would have privacy, and Curtis would have a recliner. To have a recliner was a rarity in a regular hospital room. The ICU spoiled us. We moved for the second time that evening. (Curtis wasn't very happy about toting all our stuff around for a second time and was silently cursing Teresa for all the extra decorations.) We settled into our peaceful slumber. Around midnight, I had the urge to go to the bathroom. I tried to get Curtis up to call for the nurse. I still couldn't use the call bell at this time, and he was just snoring away as usual. What could I do? I really had to go, and I couldn't hold it anymore. The suppository was doing its duty. She told me to hold for a while, and it would be easier to go. I had held it long enough. So I defecated in the bed. That was embarrassing. It was one thing to pee on yourself (you can do that laughing, and after having a close to ten-pound baby, this was a normal occurrence) but to poop on yourself? I felt like such a baby. Curtis finally woke up (I think it was from the smell) and called for the nurse who came in and got me cleaned up. Curtis and I were finally able to enjoy a couple of more hours of peaceful sleep. At about 2:00 a.m., the same thing happened again. I went on myself again. Curtis called for the nurse. I was able to wake him up this time, and in she came. One thing I'll say about Curtis in the hospital, no matter what the situation, he never complained, at least to me. I mentioned to the nurse that I was having a little bit of heartburn. My chest didn't feel right. I thought it was from the feeding tube. They'd told me I might have some acid reflux if the bed was lying too flat, so I thought it was no big deal. I thought I called a code blue, telling her that I had heartburn, because she ran out of the room to get the doctor.

A million people came into the room all at once—doctors, nurses, people off the street. They brought in a person to do a chest x-ray. A chaplain came in to pray with me. (This really boosted my confidence.) Doctors, whose names I never even knew and never saw again, were asking me all sorts of questions. "How do you feel?" "Is there pain anywhere?" "Any pressure in your chest?" All I could say was I felt like I had bad heartburn and was a little lightheaded like I had been earlier when I went through the spell where they thought I was having a seizure. There were serious looks on everyone's face, and I started to get scared. I heard murmurings of a heart attack. I thought, *Oh no, that's just great. A stroke and a heart attack?* The nurse tried to poke some blood out of me, but they couldn't find a vein to cooperate. They poked and prodded on me like I was a pin cushion. They tried up and down my right arm. They even had to bring in a special nurse who was known for her excellent blood-drawing skills to try to find a vein, and she had no success. Finally, they started looking for veins in my feet. They were putting needles in my foot. Getting a tattoo couldn't be this bad. All the while they put an oxygen mask on me, and Curtis was looking around nervously, not knowing what to do.

After much discussion among the doctors, it was decided I needed to go back to the ICU. They connected an oxygen tank to me, and back to the ICU everyone went. Poor Curtis, this was the third time we had moved all in the same evening and the third time he had to lug my stuff around. We were so tired and ready for sleep. I was wheeled into the ICU, and all the nurses who knew me were waving and commenting, "Back so soon?" so I waved and smiled back at them.

"I'm back," I said (although I knew no one understood me). I felt like a queen being rolled in her royal chariot. I had the wave down pat and everything. I finally was put onto a much more comfortable ICU bed (the regular hospital beds were awful) and poked some more. They had to put IVs back into me and do more blood work. This was just procedure upon entering the ICU. I was an old pro by now. My arms were so black and blue the next day. It looked like someone had beaten me up.

It was around 4:00 a.m. before Curtis and I got back to sleep. If we'd only known, this would be nothing considering what was to come. The storm had only begun.

Chapter 6

THE STORMS OF THE CENTURY BEGIN

THE FOLLOWING MORNING, I AWOKE with a start. I didn't know where I was. And there was this thing on my face bothering me. I realized I was back in the ICU. I saw some faces of nurses I recognized (I felt like an old soul on the ICU ward). I touched the obstruction on my face and saw that it was an oxygen mask. It was hot and sticky. I tried to take it off, but the nurse came into the room, saw what I was doing, and wouldn't let me. One of the neurological residents came by to check on me, and I wanted to know why they had sent me from the ICU to a step-down room if I apparently wasn't doing okay in the first place. Why did they let me go if they were only going to bring me back? They had given me a false sense of hope. But she couldn't understand my garbled language at all with the oxygen mask on. She got out a sheet of letters and pictures for patients who couldn't speak to point to so others could understand them (which didn't really help, by the way; it just added to the frustration). The idea was great, but the piece of paper didn't always get the point across. Like with the letter board Teresa brought in, I couldn't lift my hands high enough to actually make out a word. It made the situation more frustrating than it needed to be.

I once again tried to remove the oxygen mask so she could hear me more clearly. Like the nurse, she put the oxygen mask back on. I tried for a few minutes, again on the communication paper, and I finally gave up, exhausted from trying to get the message across. The girl left with nothing accomplished. Later that morning, my mom came in looking all frazzled. Since everything had happened so early in the morning, Curtis hadn't had a chance to tell her about the health scare and all the moving around. She thought I was in the original room they had put me in the day before in the regular part of the hospital. She had to call Curtis to find us. We filled her in on the details of the evening. Curtis and I did not want to be rude, but we were exhausted from the night before. We went back to sleep.

About 11:00 a.m., they did an MRI on me to make sure everything was functioning properly. They wheeled me down to the MRI room, put yet *another IV* in me, and put me in a big machine. It was almost like being in a wind tunnel. They put dye in my IV to show the doctors more clearly what my insides looked like and if anything wrong was happening. I wasn't scared because I'd had an MRI before. I took a good nap while I was inside the MRI machine. I've heard of many people feeling claustrophobic or bothered by the loud noise of the MRI machine, but I found it soothing and snored away. The whole situation and the lack of sleep from the night before had me already sleepy. The only part that made me nervous was the injection of the dye. When it went in, it made me feel warm and tingly all over and gave me the sudden urge to pee. *Please don't pee on the table in the MRI lab,* I thought, feeling like a little one in potty training. I held it. I'd had enough embarrassing moments already.

The rest of the week in the ICU was pretty much like the one before—rounds by doctors, baths, visitors, naps, nurses with medication. Even the physical therapist would come by and stand me up to get in a chair once a day. One day, he came in and said,

"We're going to walk today." I was very skeptical; there was no way he was going to pull this off. But we did with the help of a special walker (a Swedish walker); it was high, and I could use my arm and shoulder muscles for support. With a couple of people helping my feet and legs simulate the walking motion, I walked. It was more of a staggered walk, kind like a person who's had too many drinks, but I went all the way from my bed to the doorway and almost to the hall. I had the biggest, goofiest grin on my face. I couldn't believe what I was doing. I never imagined something as simple as walking being so hard and exhilarating. I made my way back into the room. By the time I got in the chair, I was sweating like I'd run a marathon. There were cheers, clapping, and tears of joy from family members and even some of the nurses. I was going beat this stroke that had taken so much from me. I was determined.

By Thursday, it was decided after looking at the MRI, I would go to a regular hospital room on Friday and inpatient rehabilitation Friday afternoon. In some ways, I hated to leave the ICU. That may sound weird, but it was familiar. I would feel this way about many transitions that summer. I became friends with many of the female nurses, and I was a little scared of the unknown. The nurses knew my name, and I felt safe around them. I knew that if something went wrong, they were right there. They would constantly watch my vitals and make sure I was okay. I wouldn't be watched as closely in a regular hospital room.

That Thursday, my last day in the ICU, I experienced another first: a male nurse. I knew they were out there, but I hadn't even thought about having one. *I have to hold my pee,* I thought to myself. I wasn't about to let a man clean me up. He was nice and reminded me some of my nephew, so there was a familiarity about him. I remember his name was Joe. Later in the morning, I felt the urge to go. It was now or never. I asked him for the bedpan. He acted like it was nothing out of the ordinary. As he cleaned me up, I thought, *This is weird.* No one had seen me naked before in that physical area but my husband, OBGYN, ICU nurses, and ER doctors. Okay, a lot of people had seen me naked. He was a complete gentleman, and I survived the uncomfortable situation. I admit I held it as much as I could that day. Each time, I became a little more comfortable with the situation.

Later that morning, Joe asked me if I wanted to have a bath. I'd gotten over the bedpan and letting strangers bathe me, but a man give me a bath? It was a new day and age. Here we go. As he did his job, he made small talk, made me laugh, and made it feel like it was the most common thing in the world. My mom stayed in the room with me through it all. Although I felt safe with him, I still didn't want to be alone. The bath was a success, crisis averted, and he got me in the chair. I should have used the bedpan before I got in the chair, but I didn't think about it. I suddenly had the urge to go, and I peed on myself. In a chair. In front of a guy. I was so embarrassed, but I couldn't sit in my own urine forever. (After my stroke, my ability to hold it had diminished.) I decided to tell Joe (he would find out eventually anyway), and he acted like it was nothing to get me cleaned up and back in bed. I never thought of males being so nurturing, but Joe had a special gift. I would find out that male nurses were a special breed.

As the day wore on, a physical therapist from the inpatient rehabilitation unit that I would be going to came by and introduced himself. He told me a little bit about what to expect in inpatient rehab. A rehab doctor, Dr. Kuntz, came by and assessed me, asking me a ton of the usual questions: "How high can you lift your arms? If I touch the bottom of your feet, can you feel it? Give me a big smile. Close your eyes as tight as you can." I had these tests memorized. He talked to me for a little while to see where I was cognitively and then left. Dr. Zukas, who was always a pleasure to see, stopped by and assessed me (Catholic, Methodist, Episcopalian, Baptist). The speech therapist came by and asked for some "ahs" and "uhs." He was full of: "Stick your tongue out for me." "Open your mouth as wide as you can." "State your full name." I felt like I was at the dentist. It was decided that I would have a swallowing test the following Monday.

I had been watching what I ate for so long before the stroke, and now, not being able to eat anything for over a week, I wanted to eat everything in sight.

The day dragged on. We were waiting on a bed for me in the regular part of the hospital. My parents came by to visit, and I napped. The day turned into evening. I thought I would get lucky and be able to spend one more night in the ICU. Maybe they had forgotten about me. No such luck. Around 9:00 p.m., on to a new double-occupancy room I went.

As I was transported to my new room, I breathed a sigh of relief. It wasn't as *bad* as the first one had been. *Beggars can't be choosers,* I thought. This was another step in the right direction. My mom was staying with me that night, and she had to sleep in a recliner that was right by my bed. It was almost as if she had crawled into bed with me. I was determined to get through this. I was only going to be there until late Friday, and then I would be going to rehab. *This is only temporary,* I kept saying to myself. This would be the motto I would use during much of my summer.

Friday dragged on and proved to be a very long, boring day as well. Curtis was at work. I remember Teresa came by on her lunch break and read to me from a devotional while I took a nap. She sang to me. She always made a point of coming by to see me once a day during the week. I was waiting for any second someone to come get me and take me over to rehab. Dr. Zukas came in for her daily visit around 4:00 p.m. that Friday, and she didn't have a very promising look on her face. She said that if I hadn't been moved to rehab by now, I probably wouldn't be until Monday. I quickly learned that hospitals didn't stick to a set schedule, and promises were often not kept. I had to stay in this room all weekend with a loud lady who liked to scream into her cell phone in the next bed? I begged Dr. Zukas to call in a favor to get me in there before the weekend, but she said she had no strings that could be pulled.

My mom and I huddled up for what would prove to be another long weekend. At least I had something to look forward to. Curtis was coming up after work to spend the weekend with me, and the kids were coming on Saturday. It was the end of the school year for them. They had been staying with my in-laws. Susie was going to bring them by the hospital for a brief visit. I was so excited. I hadn't seen my babies in over a week, and I had never been away from them for that long. While I was looking forward to it, I didn't know how the kids would react. Alex would be okay, but Katie had been a little taken aback when Karen was in the hospital. Would she be afraid of me?

Curtis was watching TV, and I asked for some pain medication to help me sleep. I remember holding his hand as we watched *Everybody Loves Raymond*, and I saw my left thumb move. I had been able to move my right arm and leg a little since the stroke, but nothing on the left side of my body. I thought I was seeing things. No, I saw it twitch again. I told Curtis to look at my left hand. I concentrated really hard, and my left thumb moved. I almost cried. We were both overjoyed. This was the first real movement I had seen on the left side at all. It was coming back. The doctors told me new pathways from the brain could replace the dead ones, and they were right. I watched TV as Curtis snored in the recliner next to me. During each commercial, I would move my left thumb back and forth a little, just to make sure I still could. My mom and dad were going to be elated about this when I told them the next day. I fell asleep happy, knowing I was on the road to recovery.

It was not uncommon for me to wake up in the middle of the night to use the bathroom. The fluid made me go every couple of hours. Twice a night was very common for me. I remember the nurse waking me up before shift change, around 6:30 a.m. She gave me some more medicine in the IV. I felt unusually groggy. I thought it was the pain medication making me really tired and went back to sleep. I felt like I was in a fog, almost in a dreamlike state.

When I woke up, I was by myself. I temporarily panicked. Curtis had gone to get coffee. I didn't feel right. I usually was able to lift my right hand to the call bell and almost to the top of my head. I tried a few times; I couldn't. Everything was blurry. It was like I was in a haze. I tried calling out for the nurse or Curtis, but if my voice was hard to understand before, it was really hard to understand now. I couldn't even understand myself. I thought it was pain medication that I had taken the night before that hadn't worn off. Something wasn't right.

Finally, Curtis came back, and I tried to tell him how I felt. He did not understand what I was saying. He had been having a hard time understanding me before, but now I was unintelligible. I tried pointing to the nurse, but it was like someone had put a weight on my right arm. It didn't want to lift up. I started to cry and then became really scared. I broke out into a huge sweat. My sheets became soaked. I was cold and hot at the same time. At this moment, my mom came in. She took one look at me and went to get the nurse. My arms started getting stiff and then relaxing. Stiff and then relaxing. My body started twisting in different directions. I was feeling like I had Charlie horses in my legs. I thought I was having another stroke. The nurse took one look at me and knew she needed backup. Nurses and Dr. Zukas rushed in. She said they needed to put another IV in me for an emergency CT angiography of my brain.

By this time, my body was completely out of control. I was sweating more, and my heart was racing about a million miles a minute. I was lightheaded and nauseated. I felt similar to when I was in the chair and had the scare in the ICU just the week before and also how I did at the beginning of my initial stroke. The nurses were trying to get an IV in me. Every time they would try to stick me, my arms would stiffen involuntarily, and they couldn't get a needle in my veins, despite their efforts. They had to hold me down to keep me from moving. My mom and Curtis stood at the end of my bed, looking helpless. The nurses gave me Ativan, and after what seemed like forever (I think it was only about ten minutes), I could feel my heart slow down. I wasn't hot anymore; in fact, I was kind of cool (probably from the cool air and all the sweat I had produced). My arms weren't stiffening up as much. They were finally able to get an IV in, and I was not feeling as nauseous. The lightheadedness started to go away. My body started to relax. *Another close call*, I thought. I let everyone know how I was feeling so they wouldn't panic. I said, "I'm feeling better. Sorry to scare you guys." It came out in a much plainer voice. They could understand me when minutes before, they couldn't. Everybody looked at me like I was crazy. Here I'd been, not five minutes before, my body writhing, and I told them I was fine. They all looked puzzled as if they didn't know what had gone on.

My mom and Curtis were shaken up. My speech was still messed up but better than it had been that morning. At least everyone could understand me now. The doctors wanted to do a CT scan, to make sure everything was working the way it was supposed to. They were baffled at what had happened. Dr. Bekenstein came in later in a quandary as well. He understood me fine, and I told him I felt okay. He kept scratching his head in confusion. Later that morning, they did another imaging. Apparently, the IV they had put in that morning wasn't in a good position, so they took it out and wanted to put another one in. This was supposed to be easy, putting in an IV, but the poor veins in my right arm were tired and overworked. They couldn't find a vein to work. I was past the point of pain now. I just wanted someone to get an IV in and get this test over with. I was exhausted from the morning's events. They had to call in a person who was known for being good at putting in IVs. She did it with no problem. They seemed to have one of these really good nurses who liked to stick it to you on every floor. They wheeled me into the radiology room. As they placed me on the table, I remember the technicians complaining about working on a Saturday. I thought to myself, *At least you're able to work. Stop complaining.* They talked about their lives and what they were planning to do after work. I think sometimes medical staff, when they are dealing with patients who can't speak or move, talk as if they can't even hear them. They talk above the patients, not to them. They forget the patients are human beings too. Finally, the CT scan was done. I was an old pro at this by then. I wasn't going to find out the results until later.

The afternoon flew by. Katie and Alex came to see me. I was afraid that after the morning's events, the nurses weren't going to let them come in. I almost forgot they were going to come with all the excitement of the morning. They both looked like they had aged right before my eyes. I had only been away from them for a week and a half, but it felt like an eternity. Alex was fine. He crawled right into the hospital bed with me. He gave me a big hug and rolled over like he was going to take a nap. The hospital atmosphere didn't bother him one bit. Katie's eyes were big. She was very quiet. She kept stroking my leg and saying, "Mommy," in a soft voice like she couldn't believe I was really there. I tried to reach out and touch her cheek, but I poked her in the eye instead. I still couldn't control that right hand very well. They didn't stay long, and they didn't understand most of what I said or the situation that surrounded them, but it did me a world of good to see them. It boosted my spirits. They got bored pretty quickly. As they said their good-byes and wrapped their little arms around my neck, it was all I could do to keep from losing it. Once I was sure they were gone and out of hearing range, I bawled my eyes out. I was happy to see them, but how long would it be before I saw them again? I was relieved that they had responded to me so naturally. Even if I was in the hospital, away from home, with a bunch of tubes sticking out of me, I was still Mommy.

Some coworkers came by (they were all teacher friends so they had a lot to say), as did a nephew and his girlfriend, Curtis's aunt and uncle, and even the preacher from the family church. My throat was hurting from all the strain I had put on it. A lot happened that day. Dr. Zukas came by around 5:00 p.m. with a model of the brain with her. She came to explain exactly what had happened with my stroke and where it had taken place. All those headaches I had been having the week prior to my stroke was my brain stem trying to tell me something was wrong. Not only had the hemorrhaging on the right side affected my motor functions on my left, the brain stem, which controls breathing, speaking, memory, as well as motor functions, had been affected. My stroke results had turned out so differently from Karen's because of where the stroke had taken place. She also told me that if the stroke had spread two millimeters higher, I would have been a goner. Talk about a wake-up call.

She was trying to tell me through all of this medical mumbo-jumbo that I was lucky to be alive. In fact, all of the medical statistics were stating that I shouldn't be there. I had drifted away from God, and this surely caused me to come nearer to Him.

My mom and dad left in the early evening to get some rest, making me promise not to give them any more scares that night. Curtis and I had a quiet evening of just watching TV. I didn't ask for any pain medication that night. I was honestly paranoid to take any more.

Sunday came and went without a hitch. Karen and her husband, Ben, came up for a brief visit. My mom stayed with me that evening. It was decided that Curtis and the kids would stay with his mom for the time being. It was closer to his work, and his mom could give him a hand with the kids. Plans for rehab on Monday were still a go, and I was still scheduled to have the swallowing test as well. I felt like I was ready for the test, but my mom didn't. There was something telling her, "Don't do it." I, on the other hand, dreamed about food all night. Teresa was supposed to meet us at the hospital on her lunch break to go with us to the swallowing test.

I woke up Monday morning with a renewed spirit. I was going to rehab that day, and I would be able to have food that night. Everything was looking up. Or so I thought.

Chapter 7

THE STORM WORSENS

I WOKE UP MONDAY MORNING ready for the swallowing test. The staff said the transport man would be there around 2:00 p.m. to pick me up. I was excited. I hadn't had any more of those crazy episodes. I had a good visit with Karen and Ben the day before. My dad put faith in me that I could do this. My mom and I had a good night's sleep. Everything looked positive. Around 1:30 in the afternoon, one of the hospital transporters came to take me to where I was having the swallowing test done. He brought a weird-looking contraption that he was going to transport me in. It was similar to a gurney, but also looked like a chair. He lifted me over to this new contraption and repositioned me to where I was sitting up. I still had no control over my head and upper body, so he had to strap me into place. I felt like they were going to take me to the crazy ward. I started to get dizzy, but I didn't tell anyone. I wanted my mom to go with me, and they allowed her to go as far as the waiting room. Teresa met us there.

As the transporter wheeled me down the hall, things were in

slow motion similar to when I had the other scary episodes in the ICU and the step-down hospital room. The glow of the lights seemed to really bother me. We finally got to our destination, and my mom and I were shown to a waiting room where we would stay until the people administering the test were ready for me. Out of nowhere, I was getting hot again, and the room started spinning. My heart was racing. I was there, but everything seemed like a dream; it wasn't reality. I was calling out for my mom. Using her mother's instinct, she knew when something wasn't right and when to get help. She had Teresa bang on the closed door until someone came outside to do something. They lowered the chair to a position where I was lying down. All of a sudden, a million people were over top of me, checking my pulse and blood pressure, which was soaring; giving me medicine in my IV; and doing who knows what else. Again, I felt like this was not happening and it was all just a bad dream. All I wanted was to go to sleep.

I was quickly transported back to my room and was given medicine to do just that. The whole episode lasted about fifteen minutes, like the other two episodes I'd already had. I don't remember the rest of the day. That night, my mom was with me again. She always seemed to be present when I really needed her. I spent all night moaning and crying out in pain. My body hurt from head to toe, and I didn't understand why. I remember a nurse giving me morphine in my IV and telling me I was going to be okay. She kept stroking my hand to help me feel safe. My mom told me to calm down; I was going to disturb the lady in the other bed. That was the least of my worries. I would be quiet for about thirty minutes and then be yelling out in pain the next. This continued throughout the night.

The next day, it was decided that I needed to have a feeding tube inserted in my belly and be placed pretty much on a liquid diet. It was called a PEG tube. The doctors decided I was not ready for my swallowing test. (My mom could have told them that.) But in order to put the PEG tube in, surgery would be required. I would be put to sleep during the procedure. It seemed every time my body was overstimulated, the episodes of my heart racing would occur, so everyone wanted to be very careful. I had the surgery on a Wednesday. Curtis, Teresa, and my mom were there with me. We went to a surgical waiting area and waited for the surgeons to get ready. The anesthesiologist came in and explained what would happen. He said it would take all of about forty-five minutes.

When he went out of the room, I realized that I still had my wedding band on. Since I had recently lost weight, it was really loose and I was afraid it would fall off during the surgery. I wanted to convey this to my mom so she could put it into a safe place and it wouldn't be lost. But there was a problem. My speaking abilities had lessoned since my first crazy episodes, and I was harder to understand. It wasn't as if I could just take the ring off and hand it to her. I would have to spell what I wanted to say to her. We had this routine where in order for me to spell out a word or phrase, my mom would go through the entire alphabet, and I would blink my eyes when it was the correct letter. I was trying to spell out the word *ring*, and I couldn't point to my ring finger; none of them got it. I didn't want to lose my wedding ring. I got frustrated, so I started crying. They told me it would be okay. The surgery wasn't that big of a deal. They thought I was upset about the surgery. That wasn't it at all. I was worried about my ring. That was another frustrating communication moment.

I calmed down to where I could take a nap. They were running behind on the surgical unit, and my surgeon came in to introduce himself. He was a small man, and I remember he came in singing Disney songs. I thought to myself, *This man who loves to sing Aladdin is going to put a hole in my stomach?* Soon, I was wheeled off. They gave me the good drugs, and I was off to la-la land. The next thing I remember is waking up with my throat hurting (they had removed the feeding tube from my nose), and my stomach was sore. I was groggy, and a nurse said, very matter-of-factly, "Wake up, and we'll take you to your room." They wheeled me back. I vaguely remember my mom and Curtis and Teresa being there. I didn't give them much notice. I just wanted to sleep. Then I got the hiccups.

I know everybody has the hiccups every once in a while, but I'd just had surgery on my stomach area. Hiccups, which could be painful in the first place, did not help my stomach feel better. These didn't last just for a few minutes. I'm talking about hours of hiccups on end. My mom said she never had trouble finding my room because she could hear me before she saw me. She was trying to sleep one night and prayed for my hiccups to stop so she could go to sleep. Dr. Zukas came by while I was sleeping (and still hiccupping). During the course of the day, she had hurt her foot, so she was wheeling around in a chair. (Something about rain and tacos?) I woke up, and she told me she wanted to do another MRI, just to make sure everything was okay after the surgery. That was the last thing I wanted to do, be transported. My stomach was hurting pretty bad at this point. Those hiccups were deep.

The transporters came to get me, and my mom said she wasn't going to go with me. She would just stay right there in the room and wait on me. (I think she really wanted to catch up on some sleep. She was pretty tired.) I gave her a pleading look that said, "Please come with me," but she didn't come. The transporter took me to the radiology room. I went through with it, and they wheeled me out into the hall. One of the technicians told me someone would come for me soon. All the while, my hiccups were in full blaze. When the technicians went back into the radiology room, I was in a hallway, on a hospital bed, totally by myself. I waited a few minutes thinking it might take them a little while to come and get me, but no one came. My hiccups echoed down the empty hall. I waited a little longer. I heard footsteps. I thought he was there, and relief flooded through me. Nope, just some guy delivering a package. I tried to get his attention by making eye contact with him, but he was too busy looking at his cell phone. I waited a while longer, still hiccupping.

They've forgotten about me, I thought. *No one's going to come to take me back. I'm going to spend the night, all alone, in this empty hallway, hiccups and all.* I started to panic, but it's not like I could yell or get up and get help. I knew that the act of crying made my voice stronger, so I started crying (half out of logic, half because I was really scared) and tried to scream for help. I was barely audible. Finally, because of the annoying noise the hiccups were making, a technician stuck her head out the door and said, "You're still here?" She made a phone call, and about two minutes later, a man arrived to take me back to the room.

I couldn't tell my mom about my big adventure getting the MRI. It was too much to spell out, and I was tired. Since I was safe and sound, the story could wait for another day.

As the night wore on, the hiccups would continue, and they were excruciatingly painful. They were getting deeper. I kept crying out in pain. The doctors decided on a medicine, Thorazine, that totally knocked me out. It didn't solve the problem, because when I woke up, I was screaming out in pain again. Then they would give me more, and I would go to sleep again. (I still had the hiccups.)

I wound up having the hiccups for several days. Karen, Stephanie, and Jon came by. Curtis and my mom were there, but I was only aware of their presence. I was in a fog. I was either asleep or in pain and asking for more medication if I woke up. Apparently, I had several visitors at this time. I had no clue. My mom told Karen about the hiccups, which she thought were no big deal. When she heard how deep and loud they were, she finally realized how bad they were.

By the weekend, the hiccups had subsided, and the doctors seemed to get the right dosage of medication to keep my episodes under control. I would learn later that the episodes I was having were called sympathetic storms. It was my body's way of healing itself, and in time, my brain would calm down. Needless to say, I didn't have any physical therapy that week. I didn't sit up for an entire week; I just stayed curled up in bed. Curtis wanted me up and in a chair after the storms had settled. He knew my muscles were tired, and he didn't want all the strength in them to go away. Finally, when I got to the chair, I would sit there for about an hour at a time. I still couldn't hold my head up on my own. It was too much of a strain on my neck muscles. I wouldn't stay there for long. I would cry and want to get back in bed.

It was finally decided that I was not ready for rehab; I would be transferred to a hospital where I would receive subacute therapy. It did involve some rehab, but not at a pace as fast as VCU's. It would move slower and help me get stronger for when the intense rehab started. I would come back to VCU when I was strong enough to put up with therapy for at least three hours a day. That might not seem like much, but not only had the storms taken useful time of therapy away from me, they had taken my speech and all movement. Now not only was my left side impaired, I could move nothing on my right. When I tried to speak, no more than a squeak would come out. I could move my eyes and thumbs, and that was it. I was locked in again. I had been given a little bit of hope, and it had been taken away from me. I was worse off than I was when I first came to VCU.

On July 1, a month after I first had the stroke, I was to be taken to the next step of my rehab process at Retreat Hospital, part of Henrico Doctors' Hospital, just a few blocks away. I remember getting a bath in preparation to go. For the first time in a month, I stripped out of a hospital gown and they put normal clothes on me. They also put Depends on me. I felt like a child in diapers. While I was having the sympathetic storms, a catheter had been put back in to eliminate the worry. If you have it in for long, feeling the urge to go can take a while to come back. I was afraid I would wet myself on the way.

I was excited and scared at the same time to move on in the next step of my journey. What were the nurses at Retreat going to be like? Would I like them? Would they like me? How long would I have to be there? How hard were the therapists going to make me work? Was I finally going to take a shower? The questions were endless.

Finally, two ambulance drivers transported me out of the

hospital bed onto a gurney to get in the ambulance and leave. Dr. Zukas wheeled down the hall behind me on her makeshift scooter (her foot was bothering her) to send her best wishes. Dr. Bekenstein came by the night before to say good-bye. I couldn't even wave good-bye or say thank you. They put me into the ambulance, and away we went. For the first time in a month, I went outside.

One funny story from my time at VCU: My mom didn't like to sit still. She was constantly swinging her foot back and forth or fidgeting. It drove her crazy to sit in a hospital room all day. During the times I was asleep, she would often go up and down the hall to have a change of scenery and get some exercise. She was constantly passing the nurses' station, pacing back and forth. Some of the nurses were getting suspicious. It wasn't until later we found out that some of the hospital staff thought my mom was a patient, trying to find a way to break out of the hospital. They thought she was trying to run away. If my mom knew what was good for her, she would have just kept on running and not looked back.

Chapter 8

THE RETREAT (PART 1)

AS I EXPLAINED BEFORE, RETREAT was an in-between hospital. It was not full-time inpatient therapy. They considered it subacute therapy. They would see to it that my strength was built up enough to get me back to VCU. It could be a matter of days, or it could be a matter of weeks. I hoped it was sooner rather than later. It was only about three blocks from VCU, but traveling in a city like downtown Richmond, it took forever to get anywhere. We seemed to hit red on every stoplight. My mom was holding my head very still. She was riding in the ambulance with me as we went down the old cobblestone streets. I closed my eyes, scared that a sympathetic storm would occur. I was taking medications, and they seemed to have the sympathetic storms under control, but I didn't want anything to trigger them again. The ride was like an eternity, and I tried to be as still as possible.

We finally made it to Retreat. My eyes were blinded by the sunlight as they wheeled me outside. People were going down the street, busy in their everyday lives. I envied them. We went down several halls and up a few floors on the elevator and entered the room that would be my home away from home for the summer of 2012—room number 580. Many nurses would know me by the room number and not by my name. I was in the Complex Care Unit. They placed me on my bed, and the two people from the ambulance crew left. Two nurses introduced themselves, one male and one female, and the young female nurse asked me all sorts of questions about my medical history. I was thinking, *Hello, I can't talk. I can barely nod my head for heaven's sake!* My mom did most of the talking for me. My main nurse was the male named Matthew. He was a peculiar sort of fellow. I was used to the idea of a male nurse by then, but something about him struck me as odd. He told me that the young female, Iza, was in training (I seemed to be the guinea pig in many situations), and he was overseeing her, making sure she was doing everything right. He gave us the ins and outs of the hospital, and my mom asked him what the policy was on overnight guests. He frowned and told her that they didn't really advise that. They wanted the patients to feel secure and be able to stay on their own. I got scared. For almost the month that I had been in the hospital, I had *someone* stay with me overnight. I was like a little girl with a blanket; I needed that comfort. My mom gave Matthew a look that said "Over my dead body. I'm going to stay." He got her a cot. He learned quickly not to mess with my mom. Even though there was some animosity at first, my mom and Matthew would eventually grow close.

Curtis and my mom went to tour the facilities. A nurse's aide came in and helped get me out of my street clothes and back into a hospital gown, no underwear. I found this practice to be useful but odd. Thankfully, Matthew gave me as much privacy as he could as they changed me into a hospital gown. My family came back in and sat down. By then, they had gotten my mom a cot and some sheets. Matthew reminded her that after a few days, once I had grown accustomed to my surroundings, she shouldn't stay any longer. They had what they called a pancake button, instead of a call bell, I could use if I needed help. It basically was a call bell, but it was square in shape and was sensitive to touch. All I needed to do was lean my head on it or tap it, and it would go off. The only problem was, I couldn't turn my head or use my hand to put enough pressure on it to make the pancake button go off. This guy wanted me to stay by myself? I couldn't even turn the TV on and off if I wanted to (and this place didn't have as many channels as VCU did, no TLC).

Finally, the nurses left, and it was just me and my family. This place was different. It had different staff, ways of doing things, everything. It was like we had just gotten used to VCU, gotten used to a routine, and then we had to leave. I kind of wanted to go back to VCU, just like I had wanted to go back to the ICU earlier. Once I was settled in a place for a little while, I felt comfortable and safe. Curtis finally had to leave; he would be going to work the next day, and it was just my mom and me. We kind of looked at each other, not knowing what to do next. I know it was hard on her to have a one-sided conversation with me, but she was a good sport about it. We watched TV for a little bit and settled in for what we hoped to be a good night's sleep. We asked Matthew if I could have an Ambien to sleep better (this was useful at VCU), and he said they didn't encourage the use of that drug there. (Did this guy have anything good to say about this place?) He said he could put an order in for Trazadone. It was another sleep aid without the drowsy side effects of Ambien. They wanted their patients alert for therapy. I thought, *Okay, whatever, just give me the sleeping pill!*

The night went on, just as it had at VCU. They were still flushing my PEG tube with water every two hours, just to make sure I was getting enough liquid. This simply meant they were putting water in my PEG tube, kind of like giving me a drink of water. They wanted to make sure I was getting plenty of fluids. Imagine taking in something to drink every two hours; that's a lot, and it makes you have to urinate often. At least a couple of times in the night, like at VCU, I had to do my business. I couldn't use the pancake button, so I would have to make some grunting noises to get my mom's attention so she would wake up and hit the button for me. At least once, I couldn't hold it. I think I got my mom after the fact. When the nurses came in, each time, they would have to turn on the bright lights. My mom would get up and stand on one side of the bed while I rolled back and forth on and off the bed pan to make sure I wouldn't fall off the bed. Thank goodness for hospital bed handrails. If I had an accident on myself, it was off with the old gown and on with the new. The whole procedure would take at least thirty minutes from start to finish (I wanted my privacy, so my mom would have to show the nurses out while I did my business). My mom and I were wide awake by the time they were done. Not much sleep was gotten that night.

To make things more interesting, the vampire, as I called her, came in around 4:30 a.m. to draw blood. Who does that? She had a hard time finding a good vein; my veins were still worn out from VCU. It took her a while to get the blood. I was totally awake by the time she left. I dozed until about 7:00 a.m., and the doctors and nurses came in, making their daily rounds. I took a deep breath and thought, *Here we go.* It was my first full day at Retreat, and I didn't know what was in store for me.

Chapter 9

THE RETREAT (PART 2)

I WAS MENTALLY READY TO get working, but everybody seemed to have a laid-back attitude at Retreat. Nobody was in a hurry, unlike the fast bustle of VCU. No one stuck to a schedule. The first day was full of evaluations. A lady with bug-eye glasses came in and was checking for blood clots. I wondered why since they already had several times at VCU. It was standard procedure every time someone was admitted. I had been in the bed so long, and they wanted to make doubly sure that no blood clots had formed. She said it was only going to take an hour or so, so my mom went down to the cafeteria to grab a bite to eat.

The lady took an ultrasound machine (Doppler) and went all over both legs—very slowly, I might add. It took forever. She tried to make small talk with me (which was interesting because I couldn't say much). I wanted to turn on the TV and escape reality for a little while, but I had no way to tell her. I just had to lie there, bored out of my mind, while she slowly went up and down my arms and legs. Then I felt the urge. I had to pee. I had no way of telling this woman

I had to go; I could only move my thumbs, and she wasn't used to my looks of alarm, which my mom understood. I tried to make noises, and she told me it would be a few more minutes, just to be patient. She wouldn't take the hint. I had to go. I wasn't going to make it much longer. What else could I do? I went in the bed. The woman didn't even notice. I would think she would have noticed the smell.

She finished my legs and started on my arms with the Doppler machine while I sat there in the warm liquid. Finally, my mom came back. When the lady finished and left the room, my mom could tell from the look on my face something was wrong. I looked at the pancake button, which the lady had put out of my reach, and my mom pressed it. She knew I needed a nurse for something. The nurses came in, checked me out, and the mystery was solved. I had to give it to the nurses that every time this happened, they cleaned me up as if it were no big deal. My mom never left the room again without me having a pancake button or a call bell nearby.

The day went on with little excitement. The occupational therapist, Linda, came in and asked me what I could do with my arms (nothing). She noticed my left hand was curling up into a fist, like I had arthritis. Whenever I slept, it would get worse. She said she would make me a brace to prevent the hand from being stuck in that position. Physical therapy came in next. They evaluated me as well, saw my lack of movement, and came up with a plan of action to get me moving again. I was disappointed that they gave me no exercises to do that day to work my muscles. I wasn't used to sitting around all day. The speech therapist, Elizabeth, came in later in the afternoon to do her assessment. More of the same. I really couldn't say anything, but at least she gave me some things to work on. She told me to try to say my ABCs and count to ten until I got bored repeating them. These were familiar patterns the brain was used to. Since I had already been taught these basic forms of communication from a young age, once the brain recognized these patterns, they would open new pathways so the speech would slowly come back. She also encouraged me to sing as well. The songs I already knew were familiar to the brain, and once practiced enough, something would eventually come out.

I felt that speech had gone the best that day. I felt like I had accomplished something. At least I had some homework to do. I was too tired to do any of it at the moment. I took about a three-hour nap. I hadn't really done anything that day except have people talk to me, but I was worn out. When I woke up later that evening, my mom and I watched some TV. I felt like I was watching TV with my husband. There weren't that many channels to choose from, and my mom had the remote. I didn't have enough use of my hands to put pressure on the remote keys to change the channels. That made me feel pretty useless. I was watching whatever my mom wanted to watch. That may not seem like a big deal, but it was just another example of how all of my decisions were being made by somebody else. I had no say (literally) in what was going on. I had to let someone know when I wanted to go to the bathroom, when I needed a pain pill, and which side I wanted to face in the bed. (They would turn me every two hours to prevent bed sores.) It was like all my choice-making abilities as a human being were taken away. It was difficult.

Wednesday was the Fourth of July. I was frustrated because the therapy staff was off that day. I wanted to get this ball rolling. I had been given a taste of therapy the day before, and I wanted to continue. It was almost like it stopped before we had even started. I did have a couple of things to look forward to. Stephanie was coming to see me. I was also going to get my first wheelchair. After being stuck in bed for so long, any way of getting up for a while seemed like a good idea. A new form of mobility was what I was talking about. I was excited. When they wheeled it into the room, it felt like I was getting a new car. I had a new set of wheels. They used the genie lift to get me out of the bed and into the chair. It had a special device for controlling my head, and like in a car, I had to buckle up.

They didn't want me falling out. They put a pad underneath me to make sure if I had an accident, the wheelchair wouldn't get soiled. Normal clothes were put on me (which was a chore), and Depends were added as well. (They wrinkled in the front and made me look like a boy. I kidded with the nursing staff and told everyone I saw I had grown a penis overnight.) My legs would not stay together. I tried, but they flopped to the side. It was like I was trying to be Sharon Stone from *Basic Instinct*. They took some Thera-band (a very stretchy, rubber-like material used a lot in physical therapy) and literally tied my legs together. I wasn't surprised by much these days. At that time, I was all suited up and ready for my big adventure through the hospital.

I hadn't been out of my room since Monday, and it felt glorious. I knew I looked like death warmed over as Curtis pushed me in my wheelchair, but I didn't care. I pictured myself in one of those electric wheelchairs, trying to make my way through Food Lion. Maybe I could qualify for a Hoveround. There was a little sitting garden in the hospital, and Curtis took me outside. It was nearly 100 degrees, and everyone else was sweating up a storm, but I didn't care. To me, it felt glorious. They all wanted to go inside, but not me. I wanted to bask in the sunlight. Nature called for me, and we had to go back inside. Stephanie and Teresa, who had shown up, went to get something for lunch for everybody (except me of course), and I was exhausted. I only stayed in the chair for about forty-five minutes, but it had taken everything out of me. I got back into bed and decided to take a little nap while they were gone.

I must have really been out of it, because it was late afternoon when I woke up. Teresa and Stephanie were already gone. They had decorated my room for July 4. They had put up balloons and streamers. There were American flags everywhere I looked. The room was full of red, white, and blue. They had even decorated my wheelchair with balloons and streamers. This made me smile. Leave it to Stephanie. She loved celebrating any holiday. That evening, my mom and I listened to the fireworks out the window. We strained to see them, but we couldn't. I should have been with my kids watching fireworks, or at least letting them have sparklers. Not this year. This would be a Fourth of July to remember. Off to sleep I went. I knew I needed to rest. The real work started tomorrow.

Chapter 10

FUN, UNEXPECTED

I WOKE UP THE NEXT day, ready to work. I had done my speech exercises until I was bored with them. I was a diligent student. Physical therapy was more involved that day. It consisted of lots of stretches and massaging of the legs. This was to stimulate muscles that hadn't been used in weeks. Under normal circumstances, that would have felt great, but I wanted to really work. They also put a towel under my knees and tried to get me to lift my legs up. I tried really hard, but my legs wouldn't go anywhere. The therapists lifted the legs up themselves making the movements to "wake up" my muscles. They gave me a few exercises to work on—rolling side to side on the bed, for example—but they couldn't give me much to practice on, because I couldn't do much. My mom took over many of these exercises. Speech was more of the alphabet and trying to count to ten. I was also working on trying to say my first sound, "m." I couldn't even say "mommy," too many "m's." My mouth couldn't close to make the sound. I couldn't even hum. It took many mouth muscles, and mine were too weak. She gave me some swallowing exercises to do as well. One of the hardest was sticking out my tongue and swallowing at the same time—not as easy as it sounds. I couldn't even get my tongue past my front teeth. She wanted me to practice this all day. Occupational therapy worked with my arms a little but not much. It was more arm stimulation, like with the legs, since my arms wouldn't move on their own. My left arm hurt when they tried to raise it above my head, and my left hand was stiff from nonuse. They said this was tone, and it would get better in time when I got more use out of my extremities.

My mom was probably my best therapist of all. She and my dad had been stretching out my arms and fingers before the therapists even saw me, and this was at VCU. She would move my arms and my legs. She would also make me move my head left and right as far as I could. I stopped when it hurt. My dad usually took over the hand part. He even fell asleep doing it a few times. My mom would have me doing some stretching exercises that had already been introduced to me when the therapists mentioned them. My mom had the weird advantage of learning what to do from Karen's stroke and applying it to me. It was like I kind of got ahead of the game, unfortunately, from things learned from Karen's experience. Without my mom pushing me so early, I might not have come so far.

Friday was more of the same. That was when the student nurses came in. For the most part, they were nice, but they didn't know how to properly use the bedpan. I quickly learned that to use and put someone on the bedpan was an art. Often, my mom had to clean up the mess they left behind. They would basically just give me my medicine, flush my PEG tube, and start the feedings. There was no way I was going to let them prick me. I would leave that to the professionals.

As Friday evening rolled around, my dad was coming to pick up my mom so she could go home and rest over the weekend. I knew she needed to leave, but she had been by my side for almost a month. I knew I was being selfish, but I didn't want her to go. Could I make it two nights without her? I was already bummed that they were not going to do any type of therapy on the weekends. How would I pass the time? It was decided Curtis would come stay with me on Friday night and Teresa would be with me on Saturday. Susie would hang out with me on Sunday until my mom came back. Then the week would start all over again.

Friday night was a breeze. My husband brought some movies from home, and we enjoyed some old favorites. This turned out to be suppository night. The nurses had to give me one every other day to keep me regular. How romantic. That meant my husband would be present when I had a bowel movement. We had been married for almost eleven years, so he knew what I did in the bathroom. I didn't make it a habit to go in front of him. I got the suppository, and about an hour into the movie, I had to go. As it turned out, Matthew was my nurse that night (seemed like he always had that privilege of suppository night when he was my nurse, poor thing). That was awkward—having two men help me onto a bedpan, one who was my husband and one who was a complete stranger. They situated me on the bedpan, and Matthew left me alone to do my business. (The nurses had learned by then that I liked my privacy.) Curtis turned the movie on pause, sat in the recliner beside me, and held my hand while he scanned the computer. I froze up for a moment. *I'm supposed to go. Like this?* I sat there in silence for a while, and he asked me if I was having any luck. Curtis started up a conversation. Seriously, were we going to talk right then? Even my mom and other visitors would leave the room when I needed privacy, but how could I ask my husband to leave? We were supposed to be together through thick and thin. But this was a little too thick. I asked him, "Don't you want to get something to drink?" I think he got the hint. As soon, as he left the room, I relaxed and went. By the time he came back up, I was clean and ready to watch the rest of the movie. There are just some things I couldn't do in front of my husband.

I could not get his attention to pee that night because of his snoring. He had the pancake button because I still couldn't use it. I honestly don't remember how I got through peeing that night with him. But I managed somehow.

Now, I loved my Teresa. She was family, and she was always making me laugh. She was the life of the party, and I had fun when I hung out with her. I was nervous about her spending the night on Saturday, not because she would be there, but because what would we talk about (although I couldn't exactly dominate the conversation)? What would we do? She was all excited. She came in and literally lightened up the whole room. She had taken pictures of the family, made collages, and framed them so I could see all the people I loved (she had done this back in ICU at VCU). She brought a lamp, blankets, pillow shams, knickknacks, anything to give the dull hospital room a pop of color. She rented the movie *Bridesmaids*, and we laughed through the whole thing. She gave me a manicure, pedicure, and facial. She put lotion on me and rubbed it all over my feet and legs. She painted my fingernails and toenails (the nursing staff was always commenting that my nails were painted so pretty). She told me her whole life story and then some. I should have known spending the night with her would be a breeze. Before I knew it, it was midnight, and we were acting like it was a slumber party.

One interesting thing that happened that night—things were always interesting when Teresa was there—involved the bedpan. (The bedpan seemed to provide entertainment for many and tended to break the ice.) I never thought my sister-in-law would see my goodies or anything else, but let's just say, we were closer than ever before. I needed to go in the middle of the night so she paged the nurse. I could get her attention when we were sleeping a lot easier than I could get Curtis's. One of my favorite nurses, Heidi, came in. Heidi actually started at Retreat a few days after I got there. She was a newbie like me. She said she needed help getting me on the bedpan. She was going to get one of her fellow nurses to help her. Teresa said, "Nah, I can help. No use calling someone else." Let's just say neither one of them were experts at putting someone on the bedpan. I had done the bedpan roll enough to know what to do.

Well, that was not what happened when these two tried. I don't know how, but my legs were positioned over my head, and I started to slide down in the bed. My head was being stuffed into my chest. I was like a human pretzel. The more twisted my body became, the more we all laughed. What could I do? I was at the mercy of these two nuts. I don't know how I got on that bedpan. But somehow, I did and successfully did my business.

I slept in late that Sunday morning, and Teresa left at midday. Susie arrived. I was extremely nervous. I have always had a good relationship with her (she had kept my kids for the first couple of years of their lives when I worked), but I hadn't, like with Teresa, spent much time with her on my own. When Teresa left, Susie asked if I wanted to go for a ride in the wheelchair. I nodded yes. They transferred me into the chair, and off we went. We went outside. It felt wonderful to be out. And naturally, we started somewhat communicating with each other (or at least I tried to talk). She couldn't understand much of what I was trying to say, but she understood enough to get somewhat of a normal conversation. This was easier than I had thought it would be. We stayed outside for about forty-five minutes. We finally decided to go back inside, and the nurses asked me if I wanted to take a shower. I didn't know. Part of me was nervous because I had never had a shower at Retreat before.

I had no idea how a shower was going to work. There was no way I could stand. I couldn't even sit in a chair, so I could only imagine what they were going to do. A girl named Natasha, who didn't seem to smile a lot, came in; she was the one who was going to give me a shower. She scared me and was intimidating. She took all of my clothes off (again, something I never would have thought I would experience with my mother-in-law). She transferred me over to a stretcher with a plastic bed. She covered me with a blanket—it looked like I was ready to go to the morgue—and pushed me down the hall to the shower room. A handheld shower was going to be used. She shut the door, and it was just her and me. She rolled up her pant legs and had a serious look on her face. She was ready to get down to business. She took the blanket off me (being naked in front of strangers was a regular occurrence for me by then) and turned the water on. It was the beginning of July, and I hadn't had a shower since early June. The water felt wonderful. I felt like a car in a carwash. The whole experience was heavenly. Natasha might have looked mean, but she sure knew what she was doing. When she was finished, she dried me off, took me back to the room, got me in bed, and put a clean gown on me. I felt wonderful.

All of these activities had worn me out, so I was definitely due for a nap. Susie and I dozed in peaceful silence for a couple of hours, and when I woke up, my mom was there. She had brought me some clothes from Stephanie (I needed some to work out in in therapy) and other goodies people from her home church had given her. I felt like I hadn't seen her in forever. I filled her in, as best as I could, on the weekend's activities, and she told me what she had done at her home. It was getting late by then, so Susie had to go home. I had survived the weekend. I was actually excited for the next week to start. I wanted to work on the walking and the talking, the important stuff. I didn't know what I was in for. Especially when I met Mary.

Chapter 11

THERE'S SOMETHING ABOUT MARY

I WOKE UP MONDAY MORNING fully expecting another week full of nonchallenging therapy. I didn't want to get myself all worked up and then be disappointed in my therapies as I had the week before. I was introduced to a middle-aged woman named Mary. She had short blonde hair and glasses, and I knew right away she meant business. She wasn't playing around. This was the first time she had worked with me, and she did a brief assessment to see what I could do, which was still not much. She made my legs sit up in a V position on the bed. They quickly flopped to the side. We worked on rolling, which was a necessary evil for the bedpan. I could kind of roll to the left but needed a lot of help rolling to the right. There was a way that she worked with me that was different from the way other physical therapists I had encountered had. Others were not better or worse; she was unique. She pushed me hard but with a gentle touch. She would not take no for an answer. She wanted me to do butt squeezes, where I would squeeze my butt cheeks together. I didn't even have the energy to do that. She told me that even if I couldn't do it, just to imagine that I could. She told me to imagine myself moving my arms and moving my legs and imagine myself walking. This would help tell the brain what I needed it to do. She was what I needed at the time. She was at the perfect place at the not-so-perfect time in my life.

Mary was my mentor, coach, cheerleader, and physical therapist all in one. She would congratulate me when I did well even when I had small victories (I rolled to the left side). She gave me stuff to work on (squeezing my butt cheeks, and bridges, which I grew to hate). When I was frustrated and crying because my body wouldn't do what I wanted it to, she would be there with a shoulder to cry on. While she was able to work with me, I felt I was really making some headway. She went on vacation and said someone else was going to take over in her absence. I did not feel the same connection with the other physical therapist that I did with Mary. Mary said that she was glad someone else would be able to work with me. Maybe someone new would have some new ideas to try. It wasn't his fault; we just didn't click personality-wise. He wound up repeating many of the exercises Mary had already given me. I felt like I was backtracking instead of moving forward. I didn't excel as much with him because I didn't feel the same confidence as I did with Mary. At the end of the physical therapy session, he told me to keep working, it would come in time. I went back to the room and wept. It wasn't his fault. I wanted Mary.

Nurses, many of whom had become close and dear friends by that time, heard me crying and came into the room to see what was wrong. I couldn't explain it to them, but my mom knew that my spirit had been bruised. The male physical therapist hadn't done anything wrong, but he just didn't give me the oomph I needed. I wanted Mary. I held Heidi's hand while I cried. She had a very nurturing spirit, and I had grown close to her. The male physical therapist just wasn't Mary.

Mary finally came back from vacation. It felt like it had been an

eternity and not just a few days. Who knew I would be so excited to
see a physical therapist? I was happy to see her smiling face. Between
my mom and me, we were able to explain what had happened with
the male physical therapist. She understood and was flattered that I
wanted to work with her so badly. She put me right to work, rolling,
squeezing my butt, and lifting my arms. Every time I saw her, she
would lift up my spirits by telling me how impressed she was. In
time, I could roll a little better. I could lift my arms a little higher.
I could actually feel my butt cheeks squeezing. I didn't know it at
the time, but my mom pulled her aside and told Mary how much
it meant to me to work with her. I was not originally on Mary's
caseload, but she took me on because my mom asked her. She even
came in on her days off, just to work with me. I told you there was
something about Mary.

I'll never forget the Friday Mary put me in the stander. It was a
machine I was strapped into. It looked like I was in a harness, getting
ready to hit the zip line (not even close). She explained to me I would
sit on the edge of the bed, be in a seated position, and the machine
would stand me up. When she wheeled the contraption into my
room, I thought she was crazy. There was no way I would be able
to use this scary-looking machine. She didn't give me a choice. It
happened that on that particular day, my mom and dad were there
and somehow, all my other therapists (speech and occupational)
wound up being in the room. They were excited and wanted to see
me stand. It was like I had my own little cheering section. Mary
brought in a mirror so I could see what I looked like when I stood.
I could then work on my posture, which needed some work. Mary
told me that when it stood me up, I needed to use every muscle in
my butt and squeeze those cheeks together to stand straight. They
got me strapped in and sitting on the edge of the bed. Here was my
moment of truth. She told me to pretend as if I had a dime between
my butt cheeks and squeeze my butt tight, not letting the dime go.
I needed to hold it in as if my life depended on it. She asked me if
I was ready, but again, she didn't give me a choice. On the count of

three, I rocked forward, and to my utter amazement, the machine lifted me up to where I stood. I was standing. I hadn't done this since June. There was a point in time when I didn't think this was possible. I was doing this because of Mary.

When I looked at myself in the mirror, I was flabbergasted, for several reasons. Since I had the stroke, I hadn't really looked at myself at all. I didn't have the need to. My mom washed my face and brushed my teeth and hair. It was not like I could get up to go to the bathroom, so I couldn't use the mirror. I looked so different. I almost didn't recognize myself. I had a wild look in my eyes, and my hair was a mess. I felt like I had a goofy look on my face, and my smile wasn't what it used to be. If I smiled, the smile was kind of crooked on the left side. It was as if my smile wouldn't reach to the left. My head was all wobbly because of the weakness of my neck muscles. My shoulders were at a slant, leaning down to the left; they wouldn't stay straight. As weird as it sounded, I thought I looked the most beautiful I had ever been in my life. I started crying. My mom and dad were crying. Everyone in the room was cheering and tearing up. This was a momentous occasion. It was special. I counted it up there with my wedding day and the birth of my babies. I was standing. Because of Mary.

I stood for about ten minutes, and that was my body's limit. I started sinking, and my butt was sticking out. I was hunched over. That was when Mary knew I had had enough. I couldn't hold my dime anymore. They lowered me down, using the machine, until I was sitting down on the bed. I felt a wave of relief flood through me. I was ready for a "good winter's nap," as my occupational therapist used to say. My dad who had said nothing this entire time said, in a small voice, "Can I let go of my dime now?" Apparently, he had been holding his butt cheeks together tightly the whole time I had, maybe even tighter. Everyone burst out laughing. Leave it to my dad.

As I continued to work with Mary on the stander, the Swedish walker, and briefly a regular walker, my confidence was boosted. She was great at what she did. I can't count the number of times I heard her say the phrase, "Tuck that butt in." I felt like I was doing one of my Jillian Michaels workouts. Mary not only gave me the go-get-'em attitude, she was a spiritual confidante as well. She mentioned several times when she did her devotions in the morning, she was thinking of me. She would often talk about the power of God and prayer with us. She gave me a devotional. Mary fasted for me one day. How many physical therapists did that? She not only cared for the sake of her job that I would one day walk again, she also cared for *me* that I would one day walk again.

When I was starting to talk better, I wanted to know from Mary what my prognosis was. I heard the doctors telling me I was doing a great job and my future looked bright, but I wanted to hear it from her. I trusted above all what Mary had to say. I remember the expression on her face and the tears in the corners of her eyes as if it were yesterday. I looked her square in the eye and asked her what I had been thinking for so long but hadn't been able to say aloud until now, "Will I walk again?" I had resigned myself to the fact that I might be stuck in a wheelchair for the rest of my life, but I wanted to know if I even had a chance at gaining my mobility back.

She paused, and as her eyes met mine, she said the most beautiful words I had ever heard: "Yes, you will walk again." I believed her. I would walk to the moon and back for her. Because there was something about Mary.

Chapter 12

BACK OFF!

NOT ONLY HAD I LOST the ability to walk, I had also lost the ability to speak. Since day one, everything sounded normal in my head, but nothing close to speech would come out of my mouth. That drove me crazy. In the past, I would ask Curtis how the kids were and remind him of what bills needed to be paid; I couldn't even tell my mom I didn't want to watch a TV channel. I remember that I had an itch on my nose one time. I couldn't even lift my hand high enough to scratch it. To the best of my ability, I tried pointing at my nose while I had my mom's attention. She was totally clueless as to what I needed. I just kept pointing toward my nose until finally she got it. She scratched my nose. I never knew scratching your nose could feel so good.

My mom and I had come up with our own way of communicating while at VCU. We had the bathroom thing down pat. When I said, "Pee," or pointed down there, she understood. She understood when I tried to say Babe, Katie, or Alex; or when I needed her, I usually just made some type of sound. *Home* was another word I used repeatedly that she understood phonetically and emotionally. I had learned how to sign the alphabet when I was younger, but no one else knew it. I thought for sure someone would know sign language, but no one did. My mom had the patience of a saint. I felt so helpless. I had to depend on her for all of my needs. That was a lot of pressure to put on someone.

My speech pathologist was another therapist who changed my life, and I give her credit for helping me learn to talk again. She was a short woman with dark hair and glasses named Elizabeth. When she first walked into my room, I honestly didn't know what to expect. She had an iPad with her and a very serious look about her. She wouldn't take any funny business. I was ready to speak to the world. Much to my dismay, our first session didn't consist of, "Say 'apple.' Good. Say 'banana.'" She told me to puff my cheeks out like a blowfish (I couldn't), stick out my tongue as far as it would go (I couldn't even get it to stick outside my mouth), trace my lips with my tongue (I couldn't stick my tongue out far enough to do so), and put my lips together and hum (Not a sound would come out). I noticed a pattern. All of these were simple tasks that people took for granted, and I couldn't even do them.

She gave me some homework to practice. (She was a good teacher like me, good at giving homework.) She told me to practice puffing my cheeks, sticking my tongue out, tracing my lips with my tongue, and trying to count one to ten. These were all normal patterns that I had earned from an early age; once my brain knew what I was doing, it would remember those patterns and they would become second nature again. It was kind of like relearning how to ride a bike. Every time I watched TV, during the commercial, I would practice the things she taught me until I was sick and tired of them (along with the butt squeezes).

After the first week, I could make out what sounded like a one to ten to me, but it would be difficult to understand for the average observer. I was so proud of myself. My breath support had been affected by the stroke as well, again because of that brain stem, so I would have to take a breath after every word I said, which meant it would take me longer to get a phrase out. I would count constantly, over and over again. I actually had to let Susie know when she stayed with me that I wasn't talking to myself; I was practicing. I didn't want her to think I had gone crazy.

The more I practiced, the better I got. The speech therapist came every day and worked with me. She would show me people's mouths on her iPad and have me mimic what I saw the people do and say. It took me forever to get the m's and s's. I couldn't get my mouth closed to say something like "mommy." I had a little bit of a lisp before, but I really did now. You should have heard me say, "Sally found seashells down by the seashore." Elizabeth had me read words, not complete sentences, much to my frustration, over and over. If I said the word by itself, I could do well. But when I tried to put a sentence together, everything became slurred. I couldn't get loud enough, and I was talking too fast (I'd always been a fast talker). By the end of the day, my tongue was so tired that my mom could barely make out anything I said. But at least something was coming out. My mom and I could carry on a semblance of a conversation. Not only was I standing and talking, some strength in my hands started to come back as well. I'll never forget the day I picked up the remote to the television and changed the channel. I gained enough strength in my hands to push the buttons on the remote and press the call bell. No more pancake button for me. Now, if I needed to use the bedpan, I could call the nurses' station. Control. I got a little bit of it back. It wasn't much, but I had power over what shows we watched. I could control how loud the TV was. I could call the nurses and tell them what I needed. And with time, it improved more and more. All the nurses at the nurses' station would comment, "Did Delanie just ask to use the bedpan herself? Wow, her voice has gotten a lot clearer." They couldn't believe the improvement.

I'll never forget the day when Curtis and I had our first real conversation all summer. It was a Friday, and he was going to spend the night with me. We were both tired, and my throat was killing me from talking all day. But he was surprised when I talked to him and he understood at least half of what I said. I still had to repeat myself several times, but he got it. He was impressed. Curtis was not a talker. But when he could make out what I was saying, he started talking to me and wouldn't stop. It was like all the things he had wanted to say and talk about over the summer, all the things he had been experiencing from his end, he could finally get off his chest, because I could respond to what he had to say. We talked about life (and its importance), his work, the kids, staying with his mom, and how we both really wanted to go home. It seemed like he was happy to talk not just to me but *with* me. We talked for about two hours.

One of the phrases on Elizabeth's iPad that I had to repeat was, "Back off!" She wanted me to say it loud and with some emotion. Some things that had changed about my voice were that I was soft-spoken, nasally (I constantly sounded like I had a cold), and monotonic. There was no inflection in my voice, which meant I couldn't convey emotion. I watched the girl say, "Back off," and then repeated the phrase. Elizabeth wanted it louder and with some feeling. I tried. We continued doing some more exercises, and then she left for the day. The next day, she came in, and before she could get a word out, I said, clear as day, "Back off," loudly and with emotion. Elizabeth just smiled. She was proud of me. Every time I would see her, I would tell her to "Back off." It was our own little joke. I still tell her to back off on Facebook to this day.

Another project Elizabeth had me working on was singing "Happy Birthday." My son's birthday was August 9, and it looked like I would have to celebrate with him in the hospital. My goal was to sing "Happy Birthday" to him and have it actually sound close to what it was supposed to. As I tried singing it the first few times, it was as if I were saying the words, but not singing the tune and changing the melody like I normally would. I was determined for it to sound normal. One day, Curtis, Katie, and Alex came in at the time I was having speech therapy. I introduced them to Elizabeth, and she had me singing simple songs with the kids using the iPad.

"Happy Birthday" was one of them, and "Twinkle, Twinkle, Little Star" was another. We sang some songs together, and she said I sounded better. When I wasn't thinking about it, the songs came back naturally and I would sound more normal. We even got Curtis in on the fun (and he is not a singer, so the fact that he joined in kind of surprised me).

Elizabeth was also busy working on my swallowing. (She had a lot of responsibilities.) As I mentioned before, I had a PEG tube inserted in my stomach. I hadn't had anything to eat or drink (by mouth) since June, and it was going into August. My mouth was dry and crusty. Things that my mouth would normally wash out with the help of food and water were getting all caked up in the roof of my mouth. I had to have a special solution. I was supposed to swish it around in my mouth, but for fear of aspiration, the nurses had to put it in and then quickly use a suction tube to get the liquid out, scared that I might swallow it. After a few weeks, the medicine worked and the crusty material on the roof of my mouth went away. They wouldn't let me have so much as an ice cube. I asked Curtis one day to sneak me in a cup of ice water. He did, but I didn't touch it; I was too guilty. Pneumonia was something I did not want to experience, especially if I brought it on myself.

Elizabeth gave me my first swallowing test at the end of July. We practiced and exercised, exercised and practiced. I thought I would be eating Olive Garden that very night. Stephanie and Jon were coming up that same day to visit. I thought maybe they could get me Chick-Fil-A for lunch. All I had to do was swallow, and surely I could do that.

I was nervous all morning. It was on a Thursday. The test was to take place around 11:30. My stomach was nauseous. It was a big deal. It seemed like every commercial on TV dealt with food. They finally came and got me around 11:00. They rolled me down to the second floor into a tiny room with a big x-ray camera, a computer, and a screen. They rolled me up to the screen and actually had to prop me up with pillows, as I still couldn't sit up without being supported. Elizabeth came in, along with a doctor whom I had never seen before. She had various things for me to swallow with different thickness consistencies. Some of the foods I swallowed were thicker than others. The thick ones went down slowly. Others that were thinner went down really fast.

Elizabeth started off on something of honey consistency. It was covered with a barium solution (very chalky tasting). The barium would show up on the computer screen and show her and the other doctor the path the food was taking as I swallowed. I was actually kind of scared. I hadn't swallowed food in so long. She had a little bit on a spoon, and I swallowed. It seemed to go down okay. It was just a natural reaction to swallow. I didn't have to think about it much. I was feeling a little more confident. Then she gave me a cookie that I was to take a bite of. I had to chew. This made me nervous as well. A small amount of the barium was placed on the end of the cookie. I took a bite. I chewed it up and swallowed on impulse. It came naturally. They were impressed with this as well. *I have this eating and drinking down pat,* I thought. Then came the liquid, which is of a much thinner consistency. She gave me a little on a spoon, and it seemed to go down all right to me, but when they looked at the computer screen, I could see worry on their faces. They gave me a little more. More concern. It was going down too fast, and I was aspirating, but my body was doing nothing to correct it. I was a silent aspirator. Normally, when food went down the wrong way, I would cough or clear my throat, and this allowed the food to go down the way it was supposed to. I couldn't cough; I couldn't clear my throat. It was decided I could have honey-consistency foods and no liquids—basically, a diet of applesauce and graham crackers. I was so disappointed. I always performed well on tests, and it really bummed me out that I hadn't passed this one.

That afternoon, while I was visiting with Jon and Stephanie, Elizabeth came in with a small amount of applesauce. I got a big, goofy grin on my face. I was going to eat. She wouldn't let me eat on my own. She wanted to control how fast and how much was going down with each bite, so she fed me. I felt like a baby. She even put a napkin bib on me and would wipe my mouth off when I made a mess. This drove me up a wall because of my control issues.

Day by day, my swallowing and talking were improving. I would look forward to seeing Elizabeth every afternoon, not to work on my speech, but to *eat*. My kids would come in, and I could finally say, "I love you." We had Alex's birthday in the hospital, and I was able to sing "Happy Birthday" (no Grammys were awarded) to him; I was thankful no microphone was there. Elizabeth let me have cake but no icing. I could press the call bell and call out to the nurses if I needed something. If I had to use the bathroom, I could determine when. I didn't have to get my mom's attention so she could let the nurse know. My independence was slowly coming back. At this point, I would take what I could get. And I could happily say to Elizabeth, "*Back off!*"

Chapter 13

PUSS 'N' BOOTS

SHORTLY AFTER MY ARRIVAL AT Retreat, my occupational therapist, Linda, introduced me to a new pair of boots. I had always wanted a pair of Ugg boots, but these didn't exactly fit the description I had in mind. They were blue in color and had wool on the inside. They didn't have laces; Velcro was used to hold them together. They were given to me in order to prevent foot drop. Since I wasn't putting weight on my feet, there was a possibility that my feet would deform; the boots kept the foot in a normal position and shape. I didn't want to drag my feet across the floor for the rest of my life. If I did acquire foot drop, that would require surgery and another hospital stay. I was not up for that.

At first, the boots weren't too bad. But they were hot on a 100-degree summer day. The therapists wanted me to wear them all day, four hours on and two hours off. I was supposed to wear them all night. That was when the boots started to hurt.

They would never hurt during the day, but around 2:00 a.m., I would wake up to a killer ache in my left foot. The closest thing

I could compare it to was like wearing a pair of shoes that were a little too tight all day and then have aching, sore feet at the end of the night. The doctors thought it was my foot fighting to get back in a normal position after the stroke (the left side was affected more than the right—my right foot never hurt). It also didn't help that in the past, I never wore socks with shoes and had formed a callus on the left side of my left foot. This was where it hurt the most. I would wake up in such pain my mom would leave the boot off for a few hours and then put it back on, even though she wasn't supposed to. I would love it when Curtis or Teresa would stay overnight with me. They would take off the boots and then forget to put them back on. I slept the best on those nights. I hated it that if I had to pee in the middle of the night, the nurses would notice my boots were off and scold me for it and back on they would go. They caught on to me.

I know the boots had my best interest at heart, but I hated those things. I would tell everybody who saw them that I was going to have a bonfire when I got home, and those boots were one of the first things to be thrown in the fire. They looked hideous and they felt even worse. When I was able to get in the wheelchair, they allowed me to wear tennis shoes, which basically did the same job as the boots by holding the feet in the correct position. When I got back in bed, back on the boots had to go. I would put off getting in bed just not to have to put the boots on.

There was one day when the pain was really bad. I woke up and felt like my pinkie toe on my left foot was broken. My mom took the boots off and that brought some relief—not enough though. My toe kept throbbing. I told my mom it felt like it was hurting all the way to the bone. She decided to call the nurse, who gave me a dose of Tylenol. Tylenol? I wanted the good stuff. I was in tears. It hurt if it moved just a millimeter. My toe hurt if my mom breathed on it. The toe would have spasms, and when it moved, it hurt. I finally cried myself to sleep around 6:30 a.m.

Mary, my physical therapist, checked my toe out later that day. She decided that being up and putting more pressure on my legs and feet than I had in months might be what was aggravating it. But she wasn't sure. I asked Dr. Kuntz to look at it, and he couldn't find anything. They decided to keep an eye on it in case there was something wrong. My foot never again hurt like that one day, which was weird. I was scared to put my boots on the next day, afraid that the pain would come back, but it didn't. I tried to talk everyone out of making me wear the boots, but it didn't work.

My best friend, Stephanie, and I used to love to shop for shoes. Honestly, I think we had an addiction. I would never ever make her wear these. They should have made the inventor of the boots wear them for a long period of time and let him see how it felt. I bet Puss 'n' Boots never felt like that while he was parading around in his pair of beautiful boots. I wish he would have lent me his pair instead.

Chapter 14

STOPPED UP

SOMETHING NOT TALKED ABOUT OPENLY in the hospital among bedpans is constipation. This wasn't a very pleasant topic, but it was part of what happened to me this past summer, and I feel like it needs to be addressed. Before my stroke, I was the type of person who liked to go every day. I would not start my day off right unless I had a good poop. I was like clockwork. It was the first thing I would do when I got to work in the morning. My husband and I had a weird relationship when it came to this sort of thing. He would give me potty calls from his work in the mornings, and we would even text each other while we were in the process. (I'm sure I am not the only one who has done this before.) Once I got in the hospital, all of this changed. I was lying in the bed and not moving around too much. This caused me to get stopped up. This was a problem not really addressed at VCU. It certainly was at Retreat.

I complained to my mom one evening that my stomach was upset. She felt my tummy, and it was as hard as a rock. She said to relax and let nature take its course. I didn't think much of it and went on to sleep. I woke up around midnight and felt the urge to go. They got me on the bedpan, and I did my business. I thought I went a lot. But my mom said I had barely done anything. It was gas.

About an hour later, I felt the urge to go again. I went, thinking maybe this time I had taken care of business. But I wound up doing the same thing. Nothing but gas. I went through this almost every hour that night. By the time the morning came, my mom and I were exhausted. We hadn't gotten any sleep that night. I thought for sure I would get some relief the next morning, but it was more of the same. I felt bad because my dad came up and was going to spend some time with me. But every time he came into the room, he hadn't been there for five minutes before I would feel like I needed to go again and he would leave to give me privacy. We didn't spend much time together this trip.

I didn't feel well at all. I was miserable. The nurses checked me (*there*) and said I had more that needed to come out. They asked me if I wanted an enema. I didn't really want one, but I wanted to feel better. I would do about anything at this point in time. In came the Fleet, and I waited for it to do its trick. A lot came out. I thought surely I was done. I was able to sleep for a little while.

Then came the urge again. I thought, *You've got to be kidding me.* The "best nurse ever," Rachel, came into the room. She checked (again, down *there*) me out and told me I had a lot more. I was impacted. I had heard of people being impacted before and knew they were hospitalized for it. I was already in a hospital, so now for the next step. They decided to give me a soap-suds enema, which was basically what it sounded like. They pumped my stomach full of soap suds in an effort to soften everything up so it would come out easier.

At this point, I was in tears. I didn't know what was happening, but I wanted somebody to fix me and now. Rachel said the enema should work and to wait a little while and lie on my side. Heidi popped her head in. She held my hand as I sobbed. (How many nurses would do this?) I waited and waited, but the soap-suds enema was not doing its job. They put prune juice down my feeding tube. I wound up burping it up, and it tasted terrible, but that was a no-go as well. I was so desperate at this point in time for relief. Rachel said she could handle it, but she would have to take care of it manually. What did she say? She would have to put her finger where? And do what? This didn't sound like much fun to me. I said, "No, thank you," and turned to the other side of the bed. That was my subtle way of saying to her, "You can leave now."

A few hours went by, and I was still in the same predicament. I cried to my mom to help, but there was nothing she could do. Here I was, a thirty-three-year-old mom of two, crying to *my* mom, because I was stopped up. There was only one thing to do. I sucked it up and called Rachel back in. I said, "Do whatever you need to do, but get that stuff out right now." I held on to my mom's hand and prepared for the worst. Giving birth to two children, one of which was almost ten pounds, was painful enough, but I had an epidural then. No such luck with this. Not to sound gross (although I probably already have), but it felt like Rachel was digging for gold up my butt. I would cry out in pain. Rachel felt bad, but I knew she was trying to help. I don't how long it took—it felt like forever—but finally, she got out what she needed to get out. That was the relief I was looking for.

Luckily, all this was over around 6:00 p.m., so my mom and I were able to settle in for a good night's sleep. Rachel would forever be known as the "best nurse ever" because of her skills in a time of need. I called her that every time she was assigned to me. I wound up getting impacted twice at Retreat. (Whitney, another nurse, helped me the other time the same way Rachel had.) The doctors didn't want me to get in this predicament again, so they put me on five different medications to prevent me having this problem (stool softeners and laxatives). Let's just say the odor of the room changed. My mom was frequently spraying Febreze. Better out than in.

Even though this was an awful experience, something funny did happen during this time. My poor dad made a point of coming and spending the night at the hospital so he could spend some extra time with me. But because of the predicament, that didn't happen. The nurses said there were no extra beds available, so my dad decided to stay in the waiting room all night. This probably would have been possible at a big hospital like VCU, but Retreat was much smaller. My dad stayed on his laptop as long as he could and then dozed off about 3:00 a.m. Apparently, a nurse saw him and thought he was a homeless man looking for a place to stay. She alerted security who found my dad, and he explained the situation. It all was worked out as a misunderstanding. Every time from then on, he was known as the homeless man around the Retreat hospital.

Chapter 15

THE FUNNY WARD

IF I HADN'T HAD A sense of humor in the hospital, I would have gone crazy. I succumbed to some of the worst things that will ever happen in my life, and I could either laugh or cry about it. I had my days where I would be depressed, but the days of laughing outweighed the ones of crying. This chapter mentions all the nurses and family members who kept me on my toes and turned a terrible experience into one of the best summers of my life.

I'll start with the bedpan. The bedpan always seemed to bring humor. So far, I had been lucky enough to where my bowel movements took place when Teresa was not staying with me. She stayed with me most Saturday nights, and this one Saturday she was with me was suppository day. I worried about it all day. Remember, they had given me *lots* of medication to make sure I went, so it was usually a big production when I would go. I thought, *I can't have a bowel movement in front of my sister-in-law.* She had seen them give me a bath before, but that was different. A bowel movement was so ... personal. Even if I asked her to leave the room, she'd know what I did. I dwelled on this problem all day. Then the moment of truth came. She stayed with me while I got the suppository. We waited for the inevitable.

We were watching a movie, *Taken*, and I asked to her to pause the movie. I needed to use the bedpan *quickly*. She called for the nurse and sat in her recliner, checking her texts on her cell phone. I couldn't really have a bowel movement with composure. I grunted, and she looked at me as if to say, "What in the world is going on over there?" The suppository would make me go, but it was still hard to get out what needed to get out. When I was on a bedpan in bed, it wasn't the best position to naturally go. I grunted again. She asked, "Are you okay?" I gave her a pleading look. She got the hint and left the room. I finished my deed, and then came the fun part, cleaning me up. She called for the nurse again, and the nurse came in swiftly. I still needed help rolling, and Teresa provided the help that was needed while the nurse was doing her deed. Teresa talked to the nurse like she did this every day. She talked about the bad weather we were having and how hot it was outside. All I could think was, *Oh goodness, Teresa saw my poop. How will I ever live this down?* But when the nurse left us alone, Teresa sat down and hit play on the DVD player. She never said another word. We continued on with our evening. I've always been grateful to her for this.

Teresa got used to helping me during my bowel movements, and it seemed like just another thing on our to-do list when she spent the night with me. She never made any comments, such as, "It stinks in here." But there was one night where even Teresa was driven to speechlessness (and that's hard to do). I didn't eat anything different, still the same old formula in the PEG tube. It must have been all the bowel medication that had been given to me. I went. I went a lot. I thought I had spilled out of the bedpan. By this time, Teresa had been giving me privacy when I went, and she came back in when the nurse was cleaning me up. When she walked in the door at the appropriate time, I knew that the smell had hit her directly in the face. She didn't say anything, but I could tell. She came over to my side of the bed, and I rolled over to her, trying not to laugh. I think there were actually tears in her eyes from the smell. She couldn't take it anymore. She raised her shirt and put her nose under it, trying to block the smell. She could have used a clothespin right about then. When I saw this, I burst out laughing and so did Teresa. When the nurse left, let's just say, Teresa sprayed a healthy amount of Febreze around the room. I should have provided everyone who stayed with me clothespins.

Needless to say, Teresa and I became close friends. I never knew what to expect whenever she came to stay with me. Poor thing, it seemed like every time she stayed with me, there was drama in her personal life. But I gave her credit, she did what she needed to do, and she hardly ever left my side when she was on duty. One weekend, she was not able to be there, so Susie, my mother-in-law, stayed for most of the weekend. Enough would happen this particular weekend that we would become close enough never to worry about lack of conversation again.

It was shower day for me. The nurses came in, stripped me naked (I had lost all sense of decency), and took me down to the shower room. In this case, Natasha was out, so a young nurse's aide named Dennesha was going to give me one. Dennesha had never given anyone a shower before. I could say I was her first. She lost her shower virginity with me. Usually, they would remove the sheet underneath me and leave one on top of me so that I wasn't exposed going down the hall. Dennesha decided to leave a sheet underneath me. I didn't say anything. I probably should have, but I didn't want her to feel like I was telling her what to do. Usually, the whole process took about thirty minutes.

When we got into the shower room, Dennesha was unsure of what to do. I slowly told her what usually happened when Natasha gave me a shower. Dennesha started the water, and the sheet underneath me got soaked. She proceeded to wash my body and hair, and then she remembered she forgot to get me a clean sheet to cover me up whenever we were done. She said she would get one from the supply closet and be back in just a minute. Before I could object, she left and *thought* she had shut the door. Notice I said *thought*. She left it cracked. I was thinking to myself, *I hope that door doesn't open.* Slowly, it started to open up little by little. Here I was, naked, spread eagle, and couldn't move a muscle. There was nothing I could do. It wasn't an option to hop off the stretcher and shut the door. I watched as it opened more and more. It was like time was standing still. I prayed to God no men walked by at that time. They would have definitely seen a peep show for free. The door was almost all the way open. I just shut my eyes and prepared myself for the worst. Just before the door was all the way open, I saw Dennesha's hand grab the door and shut it behind her. She'd realized what had happened. It was purely an accident, but I think we both breathed a sigh of relief. She finally got me all dried up, but I still had the sheet underneath me, soaking wet. She wheeled me back to the room. We were tracking water everywhere as we went down the hall. When we got to the room, Susie was waiting. She watched as water dripped from the stretcher. Dennesha got me transferred over to my bed, and she had to dry me again since I was still wet from the sheet underneath me. Nurses came in to give me medicine and about slipped on the wet floor. Dennesha asked me if she was supposed to take the sheet out from under me at the beginning. I said, "Yes." She hung her head and left the room. I knew I should have told her. I felt bad.

Susie and I had a good laugh about the series of events. We watched a little TV, and I grew tired. It was naptime. Susie worked on her Sudoku book and dozed while I slept. A couple of hours later, we were up and waiting for Teresa. We were trying to find something to pass the time, so we decided to do some breathing exercises with the spirometer I had. It was an instrument usually given to patients in the hospital to help with their breathing (one of the most useless pieces of hospital equipment one doctor told me; he shall remain nameless). I had to breathe in this tube, and it was supposed to improve my lung capacity; mine was lacking at the time. I was not having a lot of breath support, so they wanted me to do it so many times an hour. Susie brought it over to me. I was used to hitting about the fifty mark, but they wanted me to do it to one hundred. (It had different increments the respiratory specialist wanted me to hit.) I sucked in air a few times, hitting my fifty mark. I took a breath in, and it shot way up to one thousand. Susie looked at me and said, "Wow, that's good! What did you do to get it all the way up there?" Well, the force of air in had proceeded to let a good amount of air out down there. I had gone on myself and not number one.

She thought I had expelled some gas and was going to let it go without saying anything, but there was a really strong odor. She said, "Delanie, you didn't mess on yourself, did you?" Like a mom checking to see if a baby had soiled her diaper, she lifted my gown up to check, and she said, "Oh my! You did mess yourself!" Remember, all the medicine they were giving me to make sure I didn't get impacted again? I would say it was working—too well. I burst out laughing, and the force of my laughter pushed more out. It was like I was a squirt bottle. She quickly called for the nurse who took care of the situation. Susie and I had nothing to hide from each other from that day forward.

To make the weekend more interesting, Teresa came in the early evening to relieve Susie. Susie and I were still laughing from the weekend's events and filled Teresa in on everything that had happened. Teresa laughed with us and kept looking at my lips. I gave her a look that read, "What's wrong?" She was distracted because my lips were really chapped. She wanted to put some petroleum jelly on them to moisten them up. She grabbed a packet—they usually left a ready supply by my bed—opened it up, and applied the thin liquid before she looked at the name on the packet. As it settled on my lips, it felt different than petroleum jelly had before. I knew what petroleum jelly tasted like. This stuff wasn't thick like petroleum jelly and tasted sickly sweet. I kept pointing at my mouth, and now it was Teresa's turn to say, "What's wrong?" I kept pointing to my lips, and she finally understood that it was something to do with what she had just applied to my mouth. She picked up the package of what she thought was petroleum jelly and then she stopped. She showed the package to me. It said, plain as day, *"Lubricating jelly."* Enough said (at least it hadn't been opened and used). Teresa had a surprise tube of lubricating jelly in her present from me this Christmas.

If I ever felt out of place with my in-laws in the past, I had no reason to be so now. They knew and had seen more of me than I ever thought they would. Because of all these events, I could see Susie and Teresa as more than just family. They had become two of my closest friends.

Chapter 16

NURSES CAN BE FUNNY TOO

IT WASN'T JUST MY FAMILY that provided entertainment for me at Retreat. The staff provided it as well. There were some nurses and doctors who did not have a sense of humor. But most of them did. I would gain a close relationship with a few of them: Heidi, Natasha (who finally smiled at me), Rachel, Whitney, and Matthew. Oh, Matthew. He had been my first introduction to Retreat. Honestly, at first, I thought he was weird. I was intimidated by him. I soon realized that he was all talk and a jokester. I noticed that when he took care of me, he would do so with the gentlest touch. Even when he had to take care of me on the bedpan, he would be as discreet as possible. I learned to like him and trust him. He was one of my favorite nurses. That's not to say that Matthew didn't have a wild side.

Poor Matthew. It seemed like every time I had a suppository (here we go with the poop again), he was the nurse assigned to me. It got to be a big event for the two of us. Taking a dump meant I had a good day. On the days where these special events would happen, I would tell him I was working on a present for him, and I would let him know when I was ready to give it to him. (I was really desperate for entertainment.) When I had done the dirty deed, he would be all excited and actually thank me for the pleasure. I remember one night that my husband was staying with me and I had to put on hospital support hose to prevent blood clots. Like the boots, they were hot and uncomfortable. They were tight and hard to put on, and of course, I could not do it myself, so Matthew and Curtis had to put them on. Imagine, two grown men trying to get hose on a woman. It certainly was interesting.

There was an older nurse, I forgot her name, but she almost stepped in the bedpan after I had used it. My mom and I burst out laughing. The nurse said it wouldn't be the first time that had happened and wouldn't be the last. There was also a younger nurse, named Melanie, whom I considered a friend. We would always find something to giggle about. When she came in to work on me, she didn't know what she was in for. I was still on the medication to make me go (poop). I was always passing air, and it wasn't intentional. I couldn't help it. It was literally slipping out of me. One day, Melanie was helping me with a bedpan issue. I was rolled onto one side while she was cleaning me up. Without warning, I let one loose. You would have thought cannons had fired. Melanie and my mom literally jumped back and looked like they were startled. I started laughing, and that made me do it even more. It sounded like bullets were ricocheting around the room. Both Melanie and my mom were saying, "Delanie!" I didn't mean to, but it brought lots of comedic relief during a situation that was uncomfortable.

I've mentioned Heidi before; she was a nurse I could laugh and cry with. Teresa, Heidi, and I had many nights literally laughing at one another. On one of these nights, a volcano almost blew in my room. Because I couldn't swallow, all of my medicine was given to me through my PEG tube. My pills were crushed up for me, and the nurses would mix them with the liquid medication I was taking and pour it down my PEG tube. If I ever laughed or coughed while this was going on, it was possible that the medicine would come back up the tube and go everywhere, kind of what happens when the lid is taken off of a blender when it's still running. One Saturday night, Heidi, Teresa, and I were having one of our laughing fits, and it was medicine time. The nurse told me to calm down or she couldn't give me my medication, but I was in one of those moods where the more I tried to stop laughing, the more I laughed. I finally thought I had calmed myself down enough for the medicine to go down, and the nurse started to administer it to me. Then, all it took was one look at Teresa, and I was laughing again. I don't know what it was about her, but that girl could make me laugh about nothing. The medicine came up, up, and was almost out of the tube. The nurse administering the medication put her hand on top of the tube, trying to stop the liquid from coming out, but it was too late. It went all over my hospital gown and even got on the wall. This made us laugh even more.

There was one special nurse named Habakkuh, which was a name that came from a book in the Old Testament in the Bible. My husband never could remember her name, so he referred to her as "Chewbacca" from Star Wars. We never said this to her face. She was extremely nice but definitely eccentric. She would always call me "darling." She would tell me, "Good job, darling," if I had a good bowel movement. One time, she was putting me in the wheelchair, and that was an adventure. They had stopped putting me in the lift to get me in the wheelchair and were using a transfer board, a two-by-eight-foot strip of wood that was basically a slide to get in the wheelchair. Habakkuh didn't need that. She was like Samson. She had the strength of one hundred men. She could lift me from the bed to the wheelchair by herself. Once she got me in the wheelchair, I needed to be scooted back a little farther. Habakkuh thought that if she angled the chair backward, which it was designed to do, it would scoot me back using gravity. I don't think she knew how to angle the chair properly. She tried to push it to a tilt and made me do a wheelie. I was in the wheelchair only on the two back wheels.

I thought I would fall out, which would have been terrifying since I wouldn't be able to get back up. Teresa said I had a look of pure terror on my face. Somehow, the wheelchair didn't tilt backward enough to where I fell out, and I made it safely to the ground. Habakkuh figured out how to angle the wheelchair backward, and all was well. Close call.

Hospital humor was one way that I was able to make it during this difficult period. If I didn't have a good laugh every once in a while, I don't know what I would have done. Nurses would like to come to my room because they knew they would leave with a smile. I became somewhat of a favorite patient on the fifth floor—580 as I came to be known (my room number). I didn't complain, and I didn't say, "Woe is me." I looked at the situation I was in, dealt with it, and tried to make the best of it. I spent a total of six weeks at Retreat. It wasn't such a bad place to be.

Chapter 17

TIME TO GO

MANY PEOPLE CAME TO VISIT. Stephanie and her husband came several times, as did my sister and her husband, a friend I had graduated from high school with, and even my English teacher from ninth grade (she happened to live nearby). Former coworkers came, and extended family from my husband's side stopped by. Even my neurologist from VCU, Dr. Zukas, came by to see me. I never imagined one doctor from one hospital cared enough to check up on me while I was in another hospital. A special visit was from one of my former students. He didn't stay long, but just the fact that he dropped by meant a lot. My room was filled with balloons, cards, and flowers (which my mom was constantly rearranging). I felt loved.

My dad had gotten my mom and me some new technological gadgets to play with: me an iPad and my mom an iPhone. We became addicted. Every evening, we would both get on our devices and either read, check e-mails, or get on Facebook. I couldn't really do much at first. It took a lot to get the iPad to turn the pages when

I read. (Teresa had gotten me hooked on the *Fifty Shades of Grey* series.) I was able to browse around Facebook, but I couldn't type anything. Using the iPad was therapy in and of itself. As the days went by and the dexterity in my hands got better, I could finally hunt and peck on the keyboard. When I was able to put my first status on Facebook, I put simply, "Come see me." My wall exploded.

Most of the nurses knew me on a first-name basis. I could stand and talk a little bit more clearly, and I had some movement in my arms. I was making progress. Since this was an intermittent step toward rehab, whenever a patient progressed to a certain level, it was time for her to go.

Every other Wednesday, families were able to attend meetings where they could listen to what all the doctors and therapists had to say about the patient. I liked to attend these meetings with my family so I could hear exactly what was going on. I didn't like surprises. I felt like if I didn't go, people would be talking about me behind my back, even if they were saying something good. Everyone— doctors, therapists, nurses, and my family—had a feeling that this last meeting would be positive. Since the first weekly meeting, I wanted to be told that I could go to inpatient rehab at VCU. The next step after that was home.

As I listened to everybody talk, I was extremely nervous. My palms were sweaty, and my heart was racing. I was nervous over what they would all have to say. The head nurse, speech therapist, occupational therapist, and physical therapist said I was meeting and even exceeding all expectations. They had to rewrite their goals because I had already met them. Good news. Then, it was Dr. Kuntz's turn to assess how I was doing. I mentioned him before. He was a man in his thirties, very quiet with a good sense of humor. I liked him, and I could tell he cared. I could always count on him to tell it like it was. He was the one who ultimately decided if I was ready for VCU rehab or not, and I knew that if he thought I wasn't ready to go to rehab, he wouldn't send me. He was the rehabilitation doctor at VCU, so I would be seeing much more of him when I made my trip back over. I remember it specifically. His head was down; he was looking at paperwork. He was listening to what everyone had to say, taking it all in. When it was his turn to speak, the room was silent. I could feel the anticipation in the air. He knew everyone was looking at him. What was he going to say? I internally begged him to make my hopes become reality. Without even looking up, avoiding eye contact, Dr. Kuntz said what everybody wanted to hear. He simply said, "Rehab." I was going. I was elated.

Everybody in the room cheered. I had just won a race. I came to Retreat barely able to move or speak at all, and they brought me back to the land of the living. I was still in my wheelchair, and my speech had a ways to go, but I was in much better shape than I had been when I got there. Mary stood up and said how she hated to see us go, but this was one case in her physical therapy career that she would never forget. We had become close. We were forever linked. Mary started crying. She said she had something for me and my mom. She gave me a tank top that everyone had signed with words of encouragement. And then they gave me a gold medal (Summer Olympics 2012) for all the hard work I had done. They gave my mom a gray scrub shirt that said "A therapist" on it. It stood for "All therapist" since she had helped me in all disciplines while I was at Retreat. The therapists always said she was an honorary therapist since she did so much work with me. The staff even joked that they were going to hire her as one of the staff since she knew how to do everything. Mary and my mom had a good cry and shared a hug.

I left the conference room and went back to my hospital room feeling like I was floating on air. I was leaving. This was a long day coming. It didn't feel real. It was one step, literally, closer to home. As I thought about it, in some ways, I didn't want to go. Six weeks was a long time to be in one place. Like when I left VCU the first time, I had adapted to the way they did things. I was a little apprehensive of something new. What would rehab be like at VCU inpatient rehab? What would the therapists be like? Would I like them like I did the ones at the Retreat? I knew that I would have a roommate at VCU. How would that go? Many of the same questions that I had when I arrived at Retreat, I was asking about VCU rehab. I honestly started to get scared and didn't want to leave Retreat. I was crying. They were tears of joy and trepidation. It had become my home away from home. Wednesday was the day they decided I would leave Retreat. I figured it would take a few days for a bed to open up at VCU. Wednesday afternoon, they told me I was leaving on Thursday. That was fast.

It was my last day at Retreat. My mom, Teresa, Curtis, and Susie were busy packing up the stuff in my room. I had accumulated a lot since I had been there. There wasn't much I could do except sit back, watch, and act like a foreman. Finally, everything was in my van, and the room looked just as desolate as it had when I first came. One by one, the nurses and therapists came in and said their good-byes. There was lots of crying. They were sad to see me go but happy for the improvements I had made.

Two people from an ambulance team arrived at about 2:30 in the afternoon to transport me to VCU. They put me on a gurney and wheeled me out of the room. I waved good-bye to everyone on my way out. I saw faces I didn't know when I would see again. They got me into the ambulance, and back to VCU I went. The ride was still bumpy, but it didn't seem so scary this time. When we got to VCU, I went back through the familiar ER door onto the rehab unit. Who of all people should we meet at the elevator but Dr. Bekenstein, one of the doctors from my original stay at VCU. I said hi and waved to him. He was flabbergasted. I had been able to do neither when I left VCU originally. As we neared the rehabilitation ward, I noticed the sign near the entranceway said "Brain Injury Rehabilitation," and that made me stop and think for a minute. I had had a stroke, not a brain injury. Why wasn't I on a regular rehab unit? What were the rest of the patients going to be like? That question would be answered as soon as we went through the double doors to the brain injury rehab unit.

Chapter 18

HI HO! HI HO! IT'S OFF TO INPATIENT REHAB I GO!

I WAS WHEELED ON THE stretcher straight to my room, just like I was at Retreat. I was placed on the bed. The room was about half the size of the one I'd had at the Retreat. I had been spoiled. What was different about my arrival this time was that I had a roommate and only one TV. This was going to be interesting. My mom and Teresa stayed busy putting all my stuff up, trying to decorate the half of the room that was mine, while I sat in bed wondering what this place was going to be like. A million thoughts were running through my mind. I didn't have nearly as much room as I did at the Retreat, and they were trying to figure out where all my stuff was going to go. I was nervous. After a little while, nature called. I assumed I would be put on a bedpan, like usual. Instead, two nurses brought in a potty chair, which is basically like a toilet, except there are rails on the side and a backing to provide more stability. A bucket was placed underneath that was removable so it could be cleaned. This was a new experience for me. They stood me up, transferred me onto the chair (which consisted of pretty much pivoting on my right foot, since I still couldn't put any weight on my left), and then pulled the curtain closed and waited right outside. This struck me as odd. My roommate had a male visitor at the time. He couldn't see me, but he could hear everything I did. I thought they could at least take me into the bathroom. The two nurses were conversing as if I weren't there. They turned their backs and stood in front of me. I did my business and told them I was done. When it came to wiping, I couldn't reach back far enough behind me, so they had to do it. I had been cleaned up many times before, but there was something about having two people stand you up and clean your butt that was odd.

I was assigned a wheelchair and was responsible for wheeling around. The therapists wanted me to do it myself so I was as independent as possible. We all went to the family waiting room for a while, just to get out of the hospital room. There was not a lot of space in my room, and it felt kind of crowded. Besides, my visitors were a little loud for my elderly roommate. (Teresa was there.) I slowly wheeled myself down to the area where everyone else was. I was trying to use my feet to pedal and my arms to move the wheels, but it was not easy. My feet and arms would have to get stronger if I wanted to wheel myself anywhere. I visited with family for a while, and Dr. Zukas came to see me. She came to make sure I had made the transition okay and wanted to see how I was doing. The last time I saw her, I had been at Retreat in a bed talking somewhat unintelligibly. Now, I was sitting up in a wheelchair and my talking had definitely improved. She was impressed. After about a fifteen-minute visit, she left and some old family friends came by. It was nice to have visitors; it kept my mind off of everything.

At about suppertime (which I couldn't enjoy), everyone, except my mom, left and we went back to the room. The evening would have really been awful, except for my nurse, Becky. She was funny and liked to talk a lot. I liked her right away. She was somewhat like Teresa in that she was going to tell it to me whether I asked for the information or not. She told me all about her family—her first husband (and her dislike of him) and her grandkids. She made the evening not so bad. My mom wound up staying with me, but she'd had it lucky at Retreat with the fold-out bed. Here, all that was available was a recliner—and not a very comfortable one at that. We were so close that she was practically in bed with me! Somehow, we made it through the first night of sleep (I was lucky; I had sleeping pills).

I was awakened around 8:00 a.m. by the occupational therapist. She helped get me up, out of bed, and dressed. I wheeled myself into the bathroom and looked in a mirror for the first time in several months. I was expected to wash my face and brush my teeth. This was something my mom had done for me all summer. I thought, *How can they expect me to do all this so soon?* To my surprise, I could open up my Noxema, wet the washcloth, wash my face, open the tube of toothpaste, put toothpaste on the toothbrush, and brush my teeth. I could even brush my hair and make a decent attempt of putting my deodorant on. These were daily tasks that I had done for many years, but I hadn't done them on my own for so long. Another step toward independence.

We went into the gym, which was the main room where most activities took place. I watched everyone else eat breakfast. I still couldn't eat. When breakfast was over, it was music therapy time. Music therapy? Everybody gathered in a circle while a modern-day hippie with a guitar played a song. Everyone else was playing an instrument. They gave me some maracas. I couldn't believe what I was doing. This wasn't me. I wasn't a maraca-type of person. Honestly, I felt like a complete idiot. They were playing a remake of a Nicki Minaj song and changed the wording so it was about fishing. The idea was to get our upper body moving, but I just wasn't feeling it.

Afterward, I had speech therapy. She had me saying "ohs" and "ahs" and made me do some physical exercises that were supposed to make my core stronger to support my diaphragm. Next, I went to occupational therapy where I used a hand bike for about fifteen minutes. It was physical therapy where I really felt like I was doing something. My physical therapist was named Tracey. She reminded me of Jillian Michaels. I also lovingly told her she was the devil. (I said it *lovingly*.) She did an assessment to see what I could do. She had me use a walker, not very well, but she was the first person to really have me use one to any extent. I felt like an old granny. My back was hunched over, and I scooted across the floor. I also held onto a railing next to the wall and walked about twenty-five feet with nothing but a handrail to assist me. I was introduced to a gait belt, which was a belt fashioned around your waist. Honestly, it was like a dog leash. It allowed anyone who was working on you to grab ahold of you in the event you were about to topple over. (I came to hate these gait belts.) Tracey wouldn't fool around. She was there to get me to walk again. I took a liking to her immediately. She quickly fitted me for an AFO. This was a brace that fitted from the underside of my foot to just under my knee. My left foot was dragging a little, and this AFO allowed me to raise my foot and pick up my heel in a more natural way. My leg didn't want to bend, and with the AFO, I could walk more naturally.

My first day wasn't so bad. I was really ready for a nap by the end of the day. The next day was Saturday, but they still wanted me to work out for half the day. It was much of the same—more walking along the wall, doing swallowing exercises, and learning to get dressed myself. This was only half a day, so time didn't go by as quickly. I had most of the day Saturday and all Sunday with nothing to do. I was bored out of my mind. All there was to do was watch TV or read on my iPad. It was a long weekend. The speech therapist on Saturday said they were going to do another swallowing test on Monday, and from what she could see (she was the first to allow me to eat pudding; it was so good), she said I should pass the test with flying colors. She gave me swallowing exercises to do, and this allowed me to pass the time. I was worried about it all weekend but not as much as the first time. I knew what to expect.

On Monday, around 11:00 a.m., they came and took me down to the swallowing test area. My speech therapist came in and did the exact same thing as last time. She looked on a screen with another doctor whom I would never see again. The same results: the liquid was going down too fast, and I was silently aspirating. Solids went down fine. To my surprise, she told me I could eat lunch. What? My other speech therapist was so conservative, and this one was much more aggressive. I could eat. I remember it was country-fried chicken, mashed potatoes, green beans, and a cookie for lunch. The speech therapist sat right beside me and made sure I was taking itsy-bitsy bites and was chewing properly. I was not allowed to talk while I was eating. It was a lot of work to chew the food. This was the first time I had eaten anything in two months, and I could tell. About halfway through the meal, I was too tired to eat any more. Tired from chewing? They still wanted to keep my PEG tube in, much to my dismay, until I was eating enough to sustain myself by eating alone.

The next days were very predictable. I would be awakened at 8:00 a.m. to the doctors making their rounds. Dr. Kuntz was usually among them. Then the occupational therapist would come in and help me get dressed. Sometimes the doctors would come in while I was getting dressed. They would always knock once and then come on in, no matter what state of dress I was in. One time, I was naked and had to throw a blanket over me as I sat in a chair. Trying to talk to a doctor who knew I was naked was awkward. Another time, a nurse came in and did a butt check. She had to look at my butt to make sure I had no bed sores. Apparently, this was routine, so I dropped my drawers, and she checked it. All was well. By then, I had no shame. Each morning, my occupational therapist expected more. She even had me attempt to tie my shoes. One day, she came in and tied me to a chair with a gait belt (to make sure I didn't fall out of the chair), put my clothes on the bed, and said, "Get dressed." She left the room, and my mom had explicit instructions not to help me at all. To my surprise, with a little bit of moaning and groaning, I was able to get my shirt on. I figured out how to put one leg in my pants at a time, sitting down, and my mom steadied me as I stood up and pulled up the pants. One shoe at a time, I bent over and put them on. She told me to get dressed. And I did. This showed me that if I had the determination and willpower, I could do whatever I set my mind to. After I got dressed and ate breakfast (which I could actually partake in now), I would have speech, physical therapy, occupational therapy, lunch, usually another session of physical therapy, and then naptime. I didn't get as tired as I used to. My stamina was building up slowly but surely. It was nice to have a routine. This was something I had been missing for a long time.

Curtis would usually come up on Wednesdays (the daily drive was getting to him, so he limited his visits) to give me a shower. The brain injury rehab unit had a separate bathroom devoted just for private showers. There was a bench where I could sit and a pull-down showerhead. He would take my clothes off, get me in the shower, clean me up, and then get me dressed again. He had such a gentle touch. I never thought my husband would be giving me a shower in a nonromantic way. But it was romantic. We had had to give up our special time between a husband and a wife all summer, and it allowed us to have a few minutes where it was just us, with no one else around. He was so nice and understanding. I couldn't ask for more. Even the nurses commented on how sweet he was with me.

One thing that was embarrassing was the fact I had to wear adult diapers. At Retreat, I often went without any underwear, especially while I was in the bed. But to have to wear them all the time, it was degrading. I felt like I was potty training again. Of course, I could not go to the bathroom by myself. By then, I was using the potty chair over the toilet, and I still had to get someone to wipe me. I was wiped by my mom, Teresa, Susie, and Curtis. I know my mom wiped my butt when I was a baby, but now, it was a little different. No one ever said a word. No one complained. No one made any comments. Another thing I am extremely grateful for.

While at VCU, I had many guests. Some of the people who had

visited me at Retreat came over. Heidi came. Dr. Zukas stopped by a few times. It was nice to know I wasn't forgotten. Many of my teacher friends couldn't come; back-to-school week for teachers had started, and they were busy making plans for the year. It was weird that I wasn't with them. An old friend of my dad's whose wife died at VCU less than a year before made the two-hour trip from Lynchburg to see me. That really meant a lot. (She had been my first-grade teacher.)

My mom wasn't staying with me as much because school had started for her also. Teresa and Curtis were there with me most of the time. They wanted me to gain the confidence to stay by myself. There was a felon across the hall from me who was under police surveillance 24/7. That didn't make me feel too safe. I never found out what he did. I just made sure I never made eye contact with him in the hall. I also gained a new roommate, since the old one had been released. When she kept getting out of bed without permission setting off the alarm, which would cause the nurses to run into the room in a panic (she was wearing a helmet to protect her head), and called the nurses to get the picnic basket out from under her pillow because she couldn't sleep, my mom decided it was best if someone was with me each night. I didn't really feel safe alone.

I have to say out of all the patients in the unit, I was the one who was the most "here." This was a brain injury rehabilitation unit so people who were in car accidents and had had brain surgery were placed there. Some people didn't say anything and kept to themselves, staring off into space as drool came down their chin. Others would speak but would honestly make no sense. I felt out of place. Therapists, family, and visitors were the only ones I could talk to with any sense of clarity. I was missing human contact and normal everyday conversations. I was missing home and some semblance of a normal life.

My walking and talking were getting better. I could be understood 75 percent of the time (it was still quiet and monotonic, and I had to take a lot of breaths—though not as much as before), and I was walking with a walker. It wasn't perfect, but at least I could get around by myself. One day, many of us on the brain-injury rehab unit went on a scavenger hunt in the hospital and my physical therapist wanted me to use my walker part of the time. Now scavenger hunts really weren't my thing; I was going just to get the experience with the walker. I was overwhelmed by the environment outside of the rehab unit and in the main hospital. There were so many people, and everybody seemed to be walking so fast. I was afraid someone would accidentally knock into me and I would fall down. I had developed a startle reflex from the stroke. Any loud noise, shutting of a door, or someone talking loudly would startle me, and I would jump. It was like my mind was on sensory overload. I took it very slowly, and after a short distance, I got really tired. I began to think, *How am I going to go grocery shopping, go to the mall, or to my kids' school if I am acting like this?* Why was normal life so hard? Then I would be reminded every time I would come back to the brain injury unit that I had had a traumatic experience and "normal" to me would never be the same again.

Chapter 19

CRACKER BARREL

IT WAS FINALLY DECIDED I would be released from VCU Inpatient Rehab on Tuesday, August 26. After two and a half months in a hospital, I was going home. I wasn't going to my house though; I was going to stay with Susie, who lived about forty-five minutes away from home in Hopewell. The plan was to stay with her for a few months until I got into a settled routine and to go home with Curtis on the weekends. I was excited and scared at the same time. When I was in a hospital, I knew the routine, the people, and what to expect. It was like I was in a protective bubble. If something went wrong, the doctors were right there, just footsteps away. Honestly, I kept thinking in the back of my mind, *What if I have another stroke?* I had done research on the Internet and many websites mentioned that many people who had strokes had another one in five years. I tried not to think about it.

My physical therapist thought I was doing well enough on the walker, and I was ready to go on an outing. She took me outside some and taught me how to get out of sticky situations and tight corners. The purpose was to put me in the real world but have people there protecting me in case something went wrong. We were going to eat lunch at Cracker Barrel. I was excited to be someplace other than the hospital. I was a little scared too. What if I fell? What if I got choked up on the food? I had had another swallowing test by this time, and now I could have liquids, but not while I ate. I was beginning to become an expert at these swallowing tests. I asked my mom if she would go with me. A familiar face would help me remain calm.

The day arrived, and we all loaded up on a bus. The bus said "VCU Rehabilitation," and I felt like I was riding the short bus to school. I was embarrassed, I have to admit. But it was either this or the rest of my life in the hospital. The ride was about fifteen minutes. I kept sliding down in the seat, and it was hard to sit up straight without being buckled in. My mom asked me if I was doing okay. I lied and said, "Yes." I pondered what I was going to eat. I also wanted to do some shopping in the store, get my kids something. When we got there, I was lowered on the lift and given the walker. My gait belt was on with Tracey holding on for dear life. Showtime. I slowly made my way across the pavement and into the store. I had to step over the lip at the front door and walked into the shop. It suddenly seemed so small. It was hard to maneuver around all the items. I wanted to get to my seat quickly. It felt like all eyes in the restaurant were on us. At the hospital, if someone was on a walker or in a wheelchair, it was common. It was a hospital. It was expected. But at Cracker Barrel, with a train of walkers and wheelchairs, it was hard not to draw a little bit of attention.

We made our way to our seats. I know this sounds stupid, but just like it had been on the bus, it was hard to sit in the chairs. I was still having a hard time with my posture, and I felt like I was constantly slipping out of the chair. I didn't tell anybody about this. My speech therapist gave me water as we waited to order. I decided on the grilled chicken, macaroni and cheese, and mashed potatoes. Those had become a staple in my life by now. They were the easiest to eat. Somehow, the food at Cracker Barrel, which I always loved, didn't seem as good this time. Maybe the excitement, embarrassment, and physical activity of the day had affected my taste buds. I no longer wanted to go shopping in the Cracker Barrel store; I just wanted to get back to VCU, someplace familiar.

We finished eating and made our way out the door. My mom decided to videotape me on her phone to commemorate the outing. We headed back to VCU and to my room for a nap. I was pooped from the activities of the day. All I did was eat, and I was that exhausted? What was I going to do after a full day at home? I would soon find out.

The Sunday before I was supposed to go home, I was allowed to go to Susie's for the day; I had to be back at VCU by 8:00 p.m. that night. It was kind of like a trial run before I really left VCU for good. This was the second time I had left the hospital. It was the first time I would see the kids and everyone outside the hospital surroundings. I was excited. Susie was going to fix me spaghetti for dinner. It was going to be a great day away from the hospital.

Curtis took me out at 8:00 that morning. We wanted to get the most out of the day. After about thirty minutes, we pulled up at Susie's. Curtis had made a temporary ramp for me to make it easier to get into Susie's house. I couldn't do steps very well yet. I slowly made my way up the ramp. Katie had made me a "Welcome Home" sign. Both kids were full of hugs and kisses. I went in and sat on the couch. Okay, now what? The kids were running around the place that had become so familiar to them. Curtis sat down and watched TV, and Susie was in her normal place in the kitchen, playing Sudoku. This wasn't exactly how I pictured spending my Sunday. This was my first time out of the hospital. Wasn't something planned? I didn't let on that I felt this way.

We ate spaghetti, and we decided to sit outside for a while. We sat on Susie's back steps. Alex was running around while Katie was showing me her new skills of riding a bike. They had grown up so much over the summer. We went back inside, because it was getting hot, and I couldn't get up the back step, which was kind of tall—just one example of many of how life would change. Something so easy as walking up a step was not so easy anymore. Curtis had to literally lift me up and stand me up on the top step. I wouldn't go back outside for a little while.

When we got back inside, Alex decided to put a pair of Susie's shoes on. It struck me as really funny, Alex in a pair of lady's shoes, and I started laughing. He was cute as a button. Since the stroke, I had gained a sense of humor. When I laughed, it was a big deal. My whole body would concentrate on the laughing and forgot to hold the rest of myself up. The rest of me just kind of gave out and fell to the ground. My body couldn't support the laughing and standing at the same time. This happened a few times at therapy; I had wound up in the therapists' lap more than once, but they were trained to help people and prevent them from falling. Curtis wasn't. As I laughed at Alex, I knew what was going to happen before it did. I went down. I went down hard. I couldn't get back up. I was sitting on the floor, laughing my head off. I think I scared Curtis and Susie more than I scared myself. No matter how hard I tried, I couldn't get the strength to get on all fours and lift myself up like Tracey had trained me to do. For the second time that day, Curtis had to lift me up (I knew I killed his back that day) onto my own two feet. This raised a concern. Susie was going to stay with me most of the time during the day. If I fell on her watch, how was I going to get back up? The thought sobered us all a bit.

Like at Cracker Barrel, I was looking forward to getting back to old familiar VCU. It wasn't home, but at least I knew everybody was watching me. Teresa took me back up and stayed with me that night. It was the last time she had to stay in the hospital with me. It was kind of bittersweet. On Tuesday, my life as a patient was over. It was time for me to become part of the normal world again.

Tuesday morning, Curtis was there to grab my belongings and wheel me out the rehab door as early as possible. I was given my get-out-of-jail-free card. We were on our way to his mom's house. Before

I went to Susie's, I stopped off at my old workplace, Hopewell High School. We rolled into the main office (I was in my wheelchair) and surprised everyone. Here I had just gotten out of the hospital, my hospital bracelets were still on, and I stopped off at work? I wanted to go to my old room and get some books that were important to me out of the closet. They had to call the janitor to unlock the new elevator that had been installed in the school, since I couldn't walk up the stairs. I went to my old room, unlocked the door, and it was like going into a stranger's house. A new young boy had taken my teaching position. He had rearranged the room, my old desk, and it just felt different. I felt like I was intruding. I started going through the desk and the closet, taking out things that were of importance. As I did, teachers came by and said hello. I did my best to respond, but I was really overwhelmed by the day and didn't feel like talking.

When I was done, we got ahold of the janitor for the elevator again. I turned my keys into the main office (I hadn't been able to in June) and said my good-byes. Curtis wheeled me out the front door and back to the van. I was kind of sad leaving. I didn't know if or when I would ever be back.

We went to Susie's house and brought all my belongings into the house. We had a quiet supper, took showers, and got ready for bed. Alex and Katie had a hard time settling down from the excitement of me coming home, and they both wanted to give me just one more hug before they went to bed. Alex was being especially clingy. He kept poking his head out of his room and wanted to give me a hug. Curtis was becoming annoyed and yelled at him to go to bed. I, being the typical soft mom I was, yelled at Curtis and told him I had just had a stroke. Alex could give me one more hug if he wanted to. Curtis yelled at me that we had to lay down the law sometime or Alex was going to run all over me. I started crying. Alex started crying. This wasn't the happy homecoming I'd imagined. I finally calmed down enough to send Alex to bed and go to bed myself. This was only the beginning of the new "normal."

Chapter 20

THE REAL WORLD

IT WAS DECIDED THAT I would continue my therapy after I left VCU as an outpatient at Sheltering Arms Rehabilitation in their day therapy program. I would be there from 8:00 a.m. to 4:00 p.m., participating in four forty-five-minute sessions of therapy each day (physical therapy, speech therapy, and usually two occupational therapies). This left *lots* of downtime. I was supposed to start on Thursday, August 28. That just gave me Wednesday off when I got home to Susie's. Apparently, they didn't want me to stop my therapy for too long. That would not be good for my progress. It was decided I would be at Sheltering Arms for one month.

The first day wasn't so bad. Susie and Curtis were able to come with me. It was only for half a day. I was evaluated, like I had been at Retreat and VCU, to see what I was capable of. There was a lot of paperwork, meeting the nurse, and talking to the therapists. It wasn't too bad. And since Susie and Curtis were there, I was comfortable. The real test would be on Friday when I had to go by myself.

I woke up at 4:45 a.m. on Friday in order to get ready. Curtis went with me to the drop-off point. Susie came along as well. It was arranged so a van would pick me up each morning at 7:15 a.m. in a Walmart parking lot in Chester. I was nervous. This was the first time all summer that I would be alone. All the other times, Curtis, my mom, Susie, or Teresa had been with me. Not anymore. When the van arrived, I had a scared look on my face and my eyes started to well up with tears. I was like a kid on the first day of school, realizing that Mommy and Daddy weren't going to be able to stay with me. I felt like an invalid, getting into the wheelchair and being lifted up in the back of the van. I had seen medical transport vans like this one before but never imagined I would be in one. We took the silent thirty-minute ride—the driver didn't say a word to me—and arrived at Sheltering Arms around 8:00 a.m. I was wheeled into the "community room" and left until my therapy started, which wasn't until 10:30 for me that day. It wasn't like rehab at VCU; our schedules changed daily. Good thing I had brought a book.

None of the other patients in the room were talking much. They all stayed to themselves. There were about eight other patients in the room. I was cold, so I brought a light jacket with me. I didn't want to put it on until I arrived because it was hot outside. I tried to sling the jacket around my shoulders, and to my embarrassment, I couldn't get my jacket on. I had to ask someone to help me with it. This was another reminder of how impaired I was.

My physical therapist, Linda, scared me. She was rough and tough and wouldn't take no for an answer. I had had other therapists like her, but for some reason, I felt intimidated. Maybe that was a good thing; it made me work harder to impress her. She had me lie on a raised mat where I did some leg exercises and stretches that were supposed to help my legs and hips. Because I was depending so much on my right leg, I couldn't put much weight on the left, and from my right leg compensating, my right hip was killing me. Next was occupational therapy, where I rolled some hard putty into a ball, snake, doughnut, and several other unexciting shapes. At speech therapy, I was focusing on my swallowing skills. I still had the feeding tube in and had to rely on thickened liquids to drink. I would need to take another swallowing test in a couple of weeks. I drank several glasses of Crystal Light lemonade, making effortful swallows and swallowing with my tongue between my teeth. Every day after speech therapy, I had to pee badly.

I finally was finished for the day and arrived back at Walmart around 4:00 p.m. I was glad to see Susie. I felt such relief being in her car, knowing that I wouldn't have to be back there until Monday. At least I had a couple of days off. I had been given exercises by all the therapists, so I would have plenty to do that weekend.

Curtis and I hadn't been out on a date in forever, so it was decided that on Saturday night, we would go to dinner and a movie. Susie, once again, was kind enough to keep the kids, and Curtis and I headed out for a night on the town. We decided to eat at one of our favorite places, Texas Roadhouse. We parked and slowly made it inside. I was still on the walker at this point, so it was hard not to draw attention. I felt like such an old person, walking into the loud restaurant. (But having a walker had its benefits. The hostesses saw me and seated us before everyone else. We didn't have to wait.) I maneuvered my way to the booth and breathed a huge sigh of relief when we sat down.

We enjoyed the meal. The noise kind of bothered me. It was as if it were too much on my brain. And my startle reflex wasn't helping. Whenever a fork would hit the plate loudly, I would jump. No one else seemed to notice this, but I did. I had to go to the bathroom at the end of the meal, which normally would be no big deal, but Curtis wouldn't let me go by myself, no matter how much I pleaded. He actually talked to the manager and had the restroom blocked off so he could go in with me. This became another chance for people to stare. Curtis stood guard outside the ladies' restroom, and I did my business. (I could handle all bathroom requirements on my own now.) We made our way outside, among many a sorrowful stare. I didn't need people to feel sorry for me; I despised the looks on their faces. When we got outside, one thing we hadn't noticed on the way in was the slope of the ground. We were going up on the way in and down on the way out. As we got farther and farther along down the hill, we hadn't noticed but my walker kept going faster and faster. I couldn't walk as fast as the walker was going. My walk was really slow. But if the walker went tumbling ahead of me, down I would go. Curtis realized what was happening and started laughing. Big mistake. I was laughing hysterically by this point in time (half because I thought it was funny and half because I was scared). I could barely stand up. My legs started to buckle. I prepared myself for my face-plant on the asphalt. Apparently, we were drawing some attention, and a nice man came by and helped us to the car. It was decided we would go to the movie with me in the wheelchair.

Monday rolled around, and it was time to go back to therapy. It was much of the same. Forty-five minutes of each therapy. I was tired from getting up so early, but they didn't want me to sleep there. This wasn't inpatient therapy where I could go back to my hospital bed when I was tired. This was hard core. I finished up another day and met Susie back at the car around 4:00 p.m. We had to hurry home. The kids were starting school the next day, and we had to get them ready.

All summer long, I told my mom I wanted to be out of the hospital by the time the kids started school. She kept saying maybe I would be but not to get my hopes up. When I said something, I meant it. I was able to meet my goal. I helped Katie and Alex pick out their clothes, pack their lunches, and set their book bags out. I had even been able to go to the school and meet their teachers the previous week. We woke up at 4:45 a.m. the next day, in order to get everyone out the door. I was sad. My son, Alex, was starting kindergarten and getting on the bus for the first time. This was Katie's first day of first grade. They were both going to a new school. I was supposed to be there. Instead, I had to go an hour in the opposite direction for therapy. It wasn't fair. Even if their bus ride from the day care to school was only five minutes long, I wanted to witness it. I had never missed one of their milestones before. This was the reality of life after the stroke. I couldn't do everything I used to.

I was nervous all day long. I told everyone I came in contact with that it was my kids' first day of school. I was proud. I kept waiting for a phone call from the school saying something was wrong. I knew they would be okay, but they were my babies. No one knew how to take care of them like I did. I held my breath all day, and it was so nice to hear them running through the front door at Susie's that evening. They had survived their first day of school. I asked them both how school went and about what they did. All I got out of Katie was she ate lunch and played outside. Alex said, "Nothing." Apparently, they weren't traumatized at all.

We got settled into a routine of school and therapy. In a month's time, I went from the wheelchair to a walker, to a four-pronged cane, and finally a single-point cane. I took another swallowing test (fourth time's a charm) and was finally able to drink thin liquids. I was able to bake brownies and cornbread at therapy. I took sheets off of a bed and washed them. I was able to put dishes in the dishwasher. I could set a table. I went from having Curtis give me a shower to being able to take one on my own sitting down. I could even go to the bathroom by myself. This was a huge deal in independence and privacy. I was making steps in leaps and bounds. The doctors were perplexed at how rapidly I was improving (except for the one who said I walked like I was drunk—he shall remain nameless).

Finally, on October 25, 2012, I was finished at Sheltering Arms. I would be going to outpatient therapy at HealthSouth in Petersburg. This would only be two days a week. And it was closer to home. This meant that after several months of being in some type of hospital, I could go home and stay. No more staying there for the weekend and then having to pack up for the week to head back to Susie's. I could stay in the place where my husband and I had brought our babies home, where we had made so many memories, where I had my stroke.

As my husband pulled into the driveway at home, to stay, I had mixed emotions. I was so happy to be there, but this was where my life had changed in an instant. No longer would I be able to tell the kids, "Let's go outside," or watch them play on the swing set. Nor would I sit in my blue lawn chair and catch some rays while the kids went for adventures in the front yard. It was all I had in me to go up the front steps. (Curtis had put up some handrails for me.)

The first night we stayed at home went pretty well. The next morning, Curtis said he was going up the road to get some coffee. I thought nothing of it. I was still half asleep, and the kids were asleep, no problem. I honestly forgot about my condition in my state of sleep. About an hour after he left, I had to pee. The kids were up and playing by this point in time. I thought I would just grab the walker and go. Our bed is really low to the ground, and when I tried to pull up on the walker, nothing happened. I tried again. Still nothing. Katie saw that I was struggling and offered to help (she had really turned into Mommy's little helper since we got home). She tried pulling me up, but that didn't work either. I had my cell phone within reach and called Curtis. "I have to pee!" I yelled into the phone. He said, "Okay, okay, I'll be there in ten minutes." Those were the longest ten minutes. I didn't want to have an accident at home. Luckily, I held it, and he got home just in the nick of time.

Sunday, I tried to do my wifely duties around the house. I washed dishes, put in a load of laundry, and washed and put the sheets back on the bed. I was tired after I had done all this. I was disappointed in myself. The old Delanie would have spent a couple of hours doing more than what I'd just done. I couldn't do any more. I was so tired. I started crying. I felt defeated. Curtis just held me and told me to slow down. It would be okay. The new Delanie wasn't the old Delanie.

When I reentered the real world, I had this image of life as great with no problems. I had dreamed of being home since June. But things were not turning out as I had imagined. It was hard to do simple tasks. I needed someone to stay with me all the time, which put an extra burden on Curtis. I couldn't drive. I couldn't be left alone with the kids. I was used to being an independent person, doing what I wanted when I wanted to do it. Those days were gone. But I was determined I would get them back.

Chapter 21

HEALTHSOUTH

I WAS SETTLING INTO HOME life pretty well. Susie would stay with me at the beginning of the week, and my mom would come at the end of the week. We were busy going to doctors' appointments for everyone. The kids needed well checkups with the doctor, and Alex had to go back to the neurologist. He had absence seizures, which we had been dealing with for two years. Both kids saw a psychiatrist. Alex, in the middle of November, broke his arm, so we had an orthopedic doctor we had to go see. The kids were in school now and had started their regular routine of supper, homework, baths, and bed. Both had been diagnosed with ADHD, so they had their own medication and issues to deal with. Poor Curtis, who was the sole breadwinner now, took them to day care, picked them up after school, and was stressed out by the time he came home. I was so happy to see him when he came home and was excited to talk to him, but the last thing he wanted to do when he got home was talk. He wanted to relax. We had to work on our communication with each other (which was hard enough normally. An added "problem" was when your mom or mother-in-law was there constantly; they were spending the night too).

I had therapy to attend twice a week for forty-five-minute sessions. I had all three therapies again—speech, physical, and occupational. I needed the speech and physical. My plan of action was to stay for two hours. That wasn't bad. I really liked my speech therapist; she was really bubbly, and she liked to talk a lot (which might be why she was a speech therapist). She talked about her little girl, I would talk about my kids, and we seemed to click right away. I liked my first physical therapist too. She was very quiet, but she gave me the push I needed to get where I needed to go, which was walking with no assistance whatsoever. About two weeks into my physical therapy, she allowed me to take my AFO off, and I didn't have to wear it anymore. About a month into my therapy, they switched out my physical therapist. He was a red-headed guy from Ireland, which was interesting, but unfortunately, he had no personality at all. He did make me work hard, but he was always smacking his gum and checking his phone. He didn't push me like other physical therapists had.

Then there was Josh. He was as tall as a giant. Seriously, he seemed like he was seven feet tall. We were David and Goliath. I only had him as a physical therapist for two sessions, but he taught me a lot in that short period of time. He asked me what my goal was after leaving therapy, and I told him I wanted to walk without the cane. I was walking without the cane in the familiarity of my own home, where if need be, I could grab hold of the couch, chair, counter, et cetera. But I had grown to depend on the security of the cane in public. I didn't really need it. I would probably be okay without it, but I didn't want to take that chance. Josh took my cane away from me and told me the only way I was going to walk without it was to walk without it. I didn't need to bring it to therapy anymore. It sounded good, but could I really do it? No way to know but try. I walked around the gym of the therapy center. I was limping on my left leg a little bit, but when I didn't think too hard, I was walking normally. That was the trick: don't think; just do. Josh wasn't happy with my speed of walking. I thought I was going pretty fast, and he thought I wasn't going fast enough. He put a piece of Thera-band around me and pulled me around the gym. It was like I was the dog and he was pulling me around with a leash. I know that's a terrible analogy, but that was the easiest way to explain it.

He was going fast. Really fast. I felt like I was practically running. I got that big old goofy grin on my face. Curtis showed up at this time to pick me up. I didn't know what he would think about this big tall guy working with me. He had a big smile on his face. He liked what he was seeing. The next session I had with Josh, my mom came with me. She was impressed with him from the start. He noted that I didn't bring my cane with me that day. "Good," he said. "You don't need that thing anymore." He had me walk around the gym a few times, and he said he already saw an improvement from the day before. It was coming naturally. I had taught my brain to think of these movements as coming naturally. Some things, movements, your brain never forgets. It's amazing how it works like that. I don't see how anyone can say human beings are descended from monkeys after that display of a miracle!

After I walked around the gym a few times, Josh decided to have me walk *and* toss a ball to him and catch it when he threw it to me. I thought he was crazy. It was enough to have me walk, but to do that at the same time? No way. He started slowly, and to my surprise, I could do it. Like the walking, it came naturally. Josh was mean and made me pick up the ball when I dropped it. I concentrated really hard so I wouldn't drop it too much. When I mastered this task, he moved on to walking and bouncing the ball to each other. Again, this was pretty easy to do, but it took a lot of concentration. It took me a long time to learn to do anything while I was walking. When I was at Sheltering Arms, I was so out of breath when I was walking, I could barely talk. At VCU Inpatient Rehab, I couldn't talk while I walked. I would surely fall down. I had come a long way.

The forty-five minutes were up too fast, and it was time for me to move on to my next therapy. Little did I know this was the last time I would see Josh. I don't know if he moved to another department or what. The next time I came in, my old physical therapist, the woman, was there. That was fine. I liked her, and I didn't want to hurt her feelings by asking, "Where's Josh?" I wanted to work with him again though. I took it that Josh was one of my guardian angels, like Mary, Elizabeth, Rachel (the best nurse ever), Heidi, Tracey, Robin, Dr. Bekenstein, Dr. Zukas, Dr. Kuntz, and the many others who helped on this crazy journey. God knew whom I needed around me at each phase of my stroke healing process. Like the monkey business, how could you not believe in God at this point?

My two months at HealthSouth quickly came to an end. On December 1, 2012, I was finally done with therapy. I still had doctors' appointments I would need to go to. Some of the doctors and therapists told me it could take one to two years before I would fully recover, but the therapy part was done. The rest of it was on my own. It was up to me to continue the process of recovery. And that was just what I was going to do.

Chapter 22

UNEXPECTED BUMPS
IN THE ROAD

I THOUGHT THAT WHEN THERAPY was over, I could somewhat relax and enjoy life. That did happen to some extent, but not as much as I had thought it was going to. For the next month, I would encounter several mental/psychological challenges that I never expected. Many of my doctors along the way told me it would be a good idea to find a psychologist, psychiatrist, or counselor I could confide in, someone I could tell my troubles to without being judged. I saw a psychologist twice at Retreat and twice a week at Sheltering Arms. I thought, *I'll be okay.* I could do this on my own. I was already on Zoloft and some other anti-anxiety medication, so I would be fine. I was so wrong.

One problem was dealing with my kids, Katie and Alex. They loved me and still saw me as Mommy—they had during my entire hospital stay—but they didn't see me as an authority figure anymore. In fact, Katie told me on the day I came home from the hospital at VCU, "I can do anything I want because Mommy can't do anything about it." That broke my heart, but she was right. I couldn't do anything about it when the kids did something wrong. I needed to be able to discipline them and tell them what to do. They listened to Susie, my mom, and definitely Curtis. I don't know how many times I used the line, "I'm going to tell Daddy on you when he gets home" (which I knew was not the best thing to do). Spanking wasn't an option; when I tried to spank Alex, he would laugh at me. I didn't have enough strength to get his attention. Time-outs didn't work. My voice wouldn't get loud enough to holler at them. Taking things or privileges away didn't seem to bother them. I didn't know what to do. When my mom and Susie were at my house, I thought it was just too many chickens in the henhouse (and one rooster), and too many people were telling them what to do. When it got to the point where Susie and my mom didn't have to stay with me anymore, the kids were still acting this way. It was like I was talking to a brick wall. I knew these kids had gone through a lot the last summer. I didn't know what the answer was.

Another side effect of the stroke was I was diagnosed with the pseudobulbar affect (PBA). It was a state of the mind where one minute I was laughing hysterically, the next minute I'd be fine, and then I would be crying like the world was going to end. When my son was doing something wrong in front of me, the correct thing for me to do would be make him stop and discipline him appropriately. Instead, I would laugh, not a giggle, a laugh. I thought what he did was wrong but cute. Then when I started laughing, what did that tell my son? Mommy was laughing, so it must have been funny. Let me do it again. I knew it was wrong to laugh at him. I couldn't help it. I couldn't help the laughter from coming out. It was so frustrating.

On the other extreme, I was always an ugly crier, but I was downright creepy after the stroke. I would cry so hard it would be hard for me to catch my breath; I would be almost hyperventilating. I would wail. I had one of these crying spells back in September in front of my mom, dad, and sister. We were giving Karen a ride home while I was having one of the sad spells, and she called her husband outside so he could witness what I was doing. I was at Susie's one time when one of my spells happened, and she thought something was wrong with me. I scared her. These crying episodes lasted from thirty minutes up to an hour and a half. I could be completely over the situation that upset me, but I literally couldn't get myself together to stop crying. It was utterly disturbing not to have control of my emotions. I would say and do things that I definitely didn't mean. Things like: *Y'all would be better without me* or *the stroke should have just taken me.* It was like being pregnant but ten times worse.

Tremors were another side effect from the stroke. For no reason, my body would go into convulsions for only a few seconds, and then it would rest and return to normal. It was like when I would get chill bumps or when I got chilled, the natural reaction was to shiver. I would not even have to be cold. At first, I thought it was because I got cold and my nervous system was just in overdrive. But it would happen about every fifteen minutes or so. This was especially embarrassing when I was out in public. People stared at me as if I had a tic or something. Even my kids noticed it. If Alex would be sitting on my lap and would feel that I was having one, he'd ask me, "Are you okay?"

I hope one of my doctors will find medication to overcome these minor setbacks, but for now, I have to live with them. My family is a sight when we all get together—Karen on her cane, me walking slowly with a motorized-like gait, and my dad, who recently had hip surgery, limping. Even my mom is dealing with arthritis, so she limps too and has had to use my old cane on occasion. My dad used my walker and potty chair after his surgery. I wanted to get everything out of my house that reminded me of the stroke. I was just glad I had the stuff so my dad could use it. Teresa may have to have hip surgery in the future, and I'll just pass everything along to her. I already told her she can use my fancy cane (which she got me—pink flowers and very stylish) if she wants to.

I've been able to keep in touch with a lot of the people who were such a support to me last summer. I made an unannounced visit back to Retreat in October 2012, when I was still using the cane and saw people who cared for me. I saw Mary and was able to give her a big hug standing up. I hadn't been able to do that this past summer. I heard that it meant a lot that I came back and showed them the progress because Retreat didn't see that often. That same day, I had a doctor's appointment with Dr. Kuntz and had to go to VCU. I ran into Dr. Zukas. She hadn't seen me since VCU Inpatient Rehab, and here I was at the same hospital walking around with Susie. With no assistance. She did a double take, and then a big smile spread across her face. She came up and gave me a hug, still in disbelief at what she was seeing. It was great to let these people who had seen me in my darkest hour know I was okay.

I ran into Dr. Bekenstein at VCU in December 2012; I happened to be there for an appointment with Dr. Zukas. (I was always going to the doctor.) He was talking to two older ladies; one I assume had a stroke and couldn't walk well. Dr. Bekenstein was apparently her doctor. I interrupted them and gave him a big hug. He was surprised to see me, with nothing to assist my walking. (I don't think he recognized me at first.) I had come a long way since the last time I had seen him. I chatted with him for a few minutes and then had to get on to my appointment. As I turned to walk away, I heard one of the ladies ask Dr. Bekenstein, "Will I be able to walk like her again?" It took me a second to realize she was talking about me. That was the ultimate compliment.

Thanksgiving and Christmas 2012 had come and gone. I helped my mom with the Thanksgiving dinner and put up my own Christmas tree. I honestly couldn't believe this summer that I would have come so far so fast. The doctors call me a miracle. I shouldn't be alive. They told me I would come to a plateau, recovering very quickly, and then everything improvement-wise would slow down. It's slow moving now. I'm exercising every day. I'm seeing a counselor. I have endless doctors' appointments, but I need to eat better. I have to be on top of everything daily. It's like a job to recover in and of itself.

Overall, I'd say I'm doing okay physically. I may never return to teaching. Writing has always been a passion of mine, so I might research that avenue. Emotionally, I have a long ways to go. I had a meltdown on New Year's Eve when my husband and I were supposed to go out to dinner and a movie. I get caught up in daily life, and just when I think everything is normal, things like that happen and I'm reminded I still have a ways to go. The PBA is affecting my everyday life and relationships with the people I love. I am working with my neurologist on a new drug to help. We haven't got it down pat, but we're working on it. But with God's help, the love of my family and friends, and lots of hard work, this storm too shall pass.

EPILOGUE

IT'S BEEN A YEAR AND I'm talking to where I'm understood 95 percent of the time and walking without a cane (although I do tire very easily and I can't walk very far). My breath support and stamina still have a ways to go, but they're coming along. I am going to try the public-speaking circuit, motivating others to believe that they can do whatever they set their minds to. I speak in churches, clubs, and schools and let people know that if I made it through this long, awful journey, they can do anything they want as long as they put their minds to it.

The hardest part of my rehabilitation has been the emotional side. That is something that does not fix itself overnight. Some parts of me are better than before: I'm funny, happy, don't take things too seriously, and don't sweat the small stuff (my husband enjoys this part). Then my PBA takes over and I am like a panic-stricken young child, crying my eyes out. I am not able to control these happy and sad times, and that's what kills me. To be out of control emotionally has been one of the worst things out of this whole experience.

Another problem is feeling forgotten and not needed. If any of my friends read this, I'm not trying to get them to feel guilty. I'm just telling the truth. When I was first in the hospital, many friends and colleagues came by to see me, brought me flowers, and sent words of encouragement. Many followed me on Facebook and told me how good I was doing. When school started, they all went to work; I went to rehab. In the past, whenever my friends were going through any type of turmoil, I did my best to make sure they were okay. I'd call or e-mail them and tell them they were in my thoughts and prayers. I've received a handful of phone calls since I've been home. With the exception of Stephanie and my family, it was as if I fell off the face of the earth after leaving the hospital. I was walking and talking, so I must be okay, I'm sure everyone thought. No one ever asked if I was doing fine emotionally.

I remember going out with some former girlfriends back in October 2012. After deciding to get together at a local restaurant (I was the one who initiated the outing), I was really excited. I would get to see my friends again. We would talk about nothing that really mattered, but it would mean everything to me. When I got to the restaurant, half the people who said they were coming never showed up. One didn't want to come because it was raining. That was an excuse. I was devastated. The meal was good, and they tried to carry on a normal conversation. But I was out of the loop. They were talking about things that were happening at work—things that I didn't know anything about—and I felt like I was an outsider, looking in on their lives. They were doing that thing where they were talking loudly to me when there was nothing wrong with my hearing. I was sad. I kind of wished I hadn't come. It made me depressed. They haven't invited me out again.

Thanksgiving and Christmas 2012 were hard as well. Stephanie called and sent me a Christmas gift. She even came to the hospital when my dad had his hip replacement surgery. Other than that, I received one e-mail from a friend saying, "Happy holidays." That was it. Nothing. No Christmas cards (even though I had sent out a couple myself). I thought they might want to get together over the holidays, but they did not. I felt bitter.

I feel like out of sight, out of mind. I cry to my husband. Everyone else is living his or her life and can't seem to include me. It's as if the stroke didn't even happen. Even my neurologist, whom I had formed a special bond with, couldn't be my friend. I finally found someone I could really talk to, and all of our talking had to be in a doctor's office. I had my family, and that was about it. (But that was a lot.)

Stroke survivors may understand where I'm coming from, but for others, life after a stroke is much different than one can imagine. Forget the rehabilitation of the physical body. The mental is more important and takes the longest to heal. Here I am, the outer shell of the person I used to be, but I don't feel the same inside. The ones I love don't know how to deal with the new me, and I often feel as if my husband has to get used to this new woman. I am not the woman he married. I'm not better or worse; I'm just new.

So if relatives or friends or other people have any type of ailment or keep to themselves for any reason, keep all this in mind. Don't forget about them. Treat them as people with feelings. Don't think that because people like me are doing okay physically that we are doing okay mentally. Others don't know what is going on in my head. I am grieving my former life, and I need people to understand the changes that are taking place.

When my sister had her stroke, I didn't understand who she was. Sometimes to the extent of anger, I could not understand why the old Karen wouldn't show up. But now I understand. She was still there, but just in a different form. No matter what, she was still Karen. My mom had dubbed us "The Stroke Sisters."

Be understanding. Live life to its fullest. Pick your battles. Don't worry; be happy. I know these all sound like clichés, but I wish I had lived by these mottos before. Everything you love can change so fast.

Delanie, her dad and mom, and Karen in
June 2011 at their parents' fortieth wedding
anniversary, before anyone had a stroke

Delanie and Karen, four days before
Karen's stroke, August 2011

Karen and Delanie before Delanie's stroke, November 2011

Curtis, Alex, and Delanie, two days before stroke
at son's preschool graduation, June 4, 2012

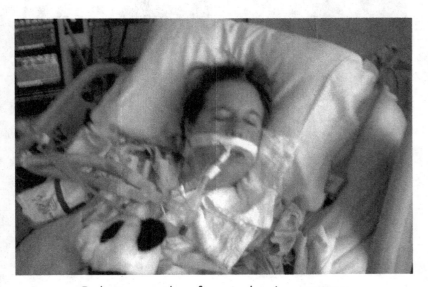

Delanie, one day after stroke, June 7, 2012

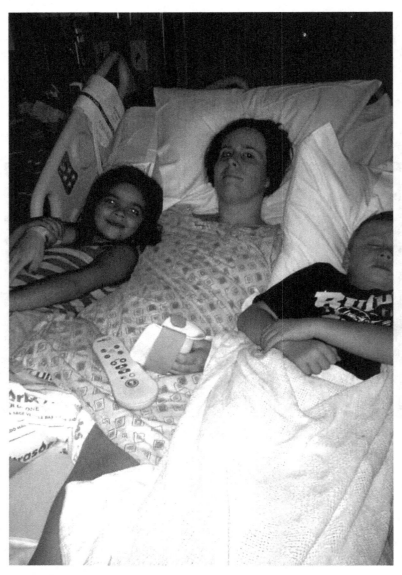

Delanie and her babies (notice Alex asleep), July 2012

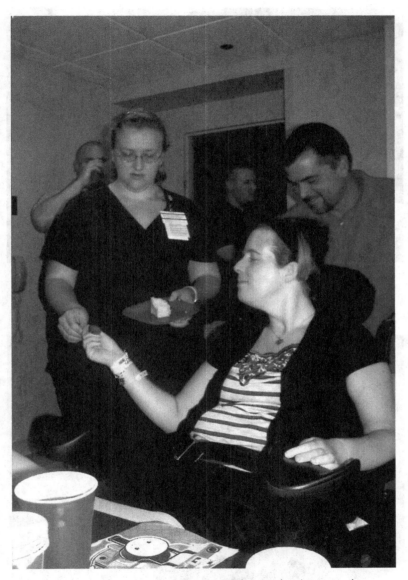

Delanie, having a nurse serve her cake (no icing)
during her son's birthday at Retreat, August 2012

Delanie and Katie, August 2012

Delanie and Karen, August 2012

Delanie and Heidi, one of her favorite
nurses at Retreat, August 2012

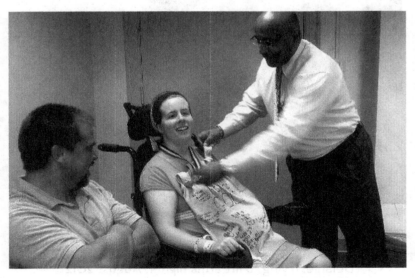

Delanie receiving her "Gold Medal" after all of her
hard work at Retreat with Greg Davis, August 2012

Delanie, trying to lift arms higher, August 2012

Learning to walk, August 2012

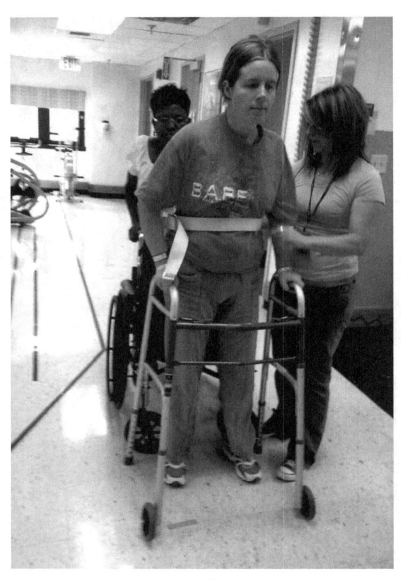

Relearning to walk, August 2012

Happy Delanie, October 2012

Delanie, first night out after going home, November 2012

Delanie and her son, Alex, November 2012

Delanie and Karen, "The Stroke Sisters," November 2012

Alex, Curtis, Delanie, and Katie, November 2012

Delanie and Curtis, November 2012

Delanie and her husband, Curtis, December 2012